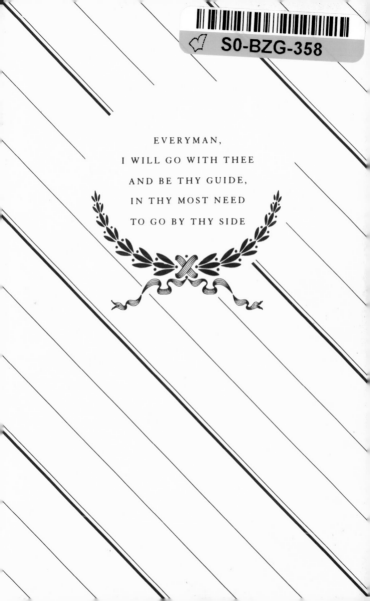

EVERYMAN,
I WILL GO WITH THEE
AND BE THY GUIDE,
IN THY MOST NEED
TO GO BY THY SIDE

EVERYMAN'S LIBRARY
POCKET POETS

Poe

Poems and Prose

EVERYMAN'S LIBRARY

POCKET POETS

Alfred A. Knopf · New York · Toronto

THIS IS A BORZOI BOOK
PUBLISHED BY ALFRED A. KNOPF, INC.

This selection by John Hollander first published in
Everyman's Library, 1995
Copyright © 1995 by David Campbell Publishers Ltd.
Ninth printing

ISBN 0-679-44505-6
LC 95-15329

Library of Congress Cataloging-in-Publication Data
Poe, Edgar Allan, 1809-1849.
Poems / Edgar Allan Poe
p.   cm. – (Everyman's library pocket poets)
Includes index.
ISBN 0-679-44505-6
1. Fantastic poetry, American.   1. Title   II. Series.
PS2605.A1 1995a   95-15329
811'.3–dc20   CIP

Typography by Peter B. Willberg

Typeset in the UK by Acc Computing, Queen Camel, Somerset

Printed and bound in Germany
by GGP Media, Pössneck

EDGAR ALLAN POE

CONTENTS

SELECTED POEMS

INTRODUCTION

Romance, who loves to nod and sing,
With drowsy head and folded wing,
Among the green leaves as they shake
Far down within some shadowy lake,
To me a painted paroquet
Hath been – a most familiar bird –
Taught me my alphabet to say –
To lisp my very earliest word
While in the wild-wood I did lie
A child – with a most knowing eye.

Succeeding years, too wild for song,
Then roll'd like tropic storms along,
Where, tho' the garish lights that fly
Dying along the troubled sky,
Lay bare, thro' vistas thunder-riven,
The blackness of the general Heaven,
That very blackness yet doth fling
Light on the lightning's silver wing.

For, being an idle boy lang syne,
Who read Anacreon, and drank wine,
I early found Anacreon rhymes
Were almost passionate sometimes –
And by strange alchemy of brain

His pleasures always turn'd to pain –
His naivete to wild desire –
His wit to love – his wine to fire –
And so, being young and dipt in folly
I fell in love with melancholy,
And used to throw my earthly rest
And quiet all away in jest –
I could not love except where Death
Was mingling his with Beauty's breath –
Or Hymen, Time, and Destiny
Were stalking between her and me.

O, then the eternal Condor years
So shook the very Heavens on high,
With tumult as they thunder'd by;
I had no time for idle cares,
Thro' gazing on the unquiet sky!
Or if an hour with calmer wing
Its down did on my spirit fling,
That little hour with lyre and rhyme
To while away – forbidden thing!
My heart half fear'd to be a crime
Unless it trembled with the string.

But *now* my soul hath too much room –
Gone are the glory and the gloom –
The black hath mellow'd into grey,
And all the fires are fading away.

My draught of passion hath been deep –
I revell'd, and I now would sleep –
And after-drunkenness of soul
Succeeds the glories of the bowl –
An idle longing night and day
To dream my very life away.

But dreams – of those who dream as I,
Aspiringly, are damned, and die:
Yet should I swear I mean alone,
By notes so very shrilly blown,
To break upon Time's monotone,
While yet my vapid joy and grief
Are tintless of the yellow leaf –
Why not an imp the greybeard hath,
Will shake his shadow in my path –
And even the greybeard will o'erlook
Connivingly my dreaming-book.

ROMANCE

Romance, who loves to nod and sing,
With drowsy head and folded wing,
Among the green leaves as they shake
Far down within some shadowy lake,
To me a painted paroquet
Hath been — a most familiar bird —
Taught me my alphabet to say —
To lisp my very earliest word
While in the wild wood I did lie,
A child — with a most knowing eye.

Of late, eternal Condor years
So shake the very Heaven on high
With tumult as they thunder by,
I have no time for idle cares
Through gazing on the unquiet sky.
And when an hour with calmer wings
Its down upon my spirit flings —
That little time with lyre and rhyme
To while away — forbidden things!
My heart would feel to be a crime
Unless it trembled with the strings.

THE SLEEPER

At midnight, in the month of June,
I stand beneath the mystic moon.
An opiate vapour, dewy, dim,
Exhales from out her golden rim,
And, softly dripping, drop by drop,
Upon the quiet mountain top,
Steals drowsily and musically
Into the universal valley.
The rosemary nods upon the grave;
The lily lolls upon the wave;
Wrapping the fog about its breast,
The ruin moulders into rest;
Looking like Lethë, see! the lake
A conscious slumber seems to take,
And would not, for the world, awake.
All Beauty sleeps! – and lo! where lies
Irenë, with her Destinies!

Oh, lady bright! can it be right –
This window open to the night?
The wanton airs, from the tree-top,
Laughingly through the lattice drop –
The bodiless airs, a wizard rout,
Flit through thy chamber in and out,
And wave the curtain canopy

So fitfully — so fearfully —
Above the closed and fringéd lid
'Neath which thy slumb'ring soul lies hid,
That, o'er the floor and down the wall,
Like ghosts the shadows rise and fall!
Oh, lady dear, hast thou no fear?
Why and what are thou dreaming here?
Sure thou art come o'er far-off seas,
A wonder to these garden trees!
Strange is thy pallor! strange thy dress!
Strange, above all, thy length of tress,
And this all solemn silentness!

The lady sleeps! Oh, may her sleep,
Which is enduring, so be deep!
Heaven have her in its sacred keep!
This chamber changed for one more holy,
This bed for one more melancholy,
I pray to God that she may lie
Forever with unopened eye,
While the pale sheeted ghosts go by!

My love, she sleeps! Oh, may her sleep,
As it is lasting, so be deep!
Soft may the worms about her creep!
Far in the forest, dim and old,
For her may some tall vault unfold —

Some vault that oft hath flung its black
And wingéd pannels fluttering back,
Triumphant, o'er the crested palls,
Of her grand family funerals –
Some sepulchre, remote, alone,
Against whose portal she hath thrown,
In childhood, many an idle stone –
Some tomb from out whose sounding door
She ne'er shall force an echo more,
Thrilling to think, poor child of sin!
It was the dead who groaned within.

TO HELEN (I)

Helen, thy beauty is to me
   Like those Nicéan barks of yore,
That gently, o'er a perfumed sea,
   The weary, way-worn wanderer bore
   To his own native shore.

On desperate seas long wont to roam,
   Thy hyacinth hair, thy classic face,
Thy Naiad airs have brought me home
   To the glory that was Greece,
   And the grandeur that was Rome.

Lo! in yon brilliant window-niche
   How statue-like I see thee stand,
The agate lamp within thy hand!
   Ah, Psyche, from the regions which
   Are Holy-Land!

TO HELEN (II)

I saw thee once – once only – years ago:
I must not say *how* many – but *not* many.
It was a July midnight; and from out
A full-orbed moon, that, like thine own soul, soaring,
Sought a precipitate pathway up through heaven,
There fell a silvery-silken veil of light,
With quietude, and sultriness, and slumber,
Upon the upturn'd faces of a thousand
Roses that grew in an enchanted garden,
Where no wind dared to stir, unless on tiptoe –
Fell on the upturn'd faces of these roses
That gave out, in return for the love-light,
Their odorous souls in an ecstatic death –
Fell on the upturn'd faces of these roses
That smiled and died in this parterre, enchanted
By thee, and by the poetry of thy presence.

Clad all in white, upon a violet bank
I saw thee half reclining; while the moon
Fell on the upturn'd faces of the roses,
And on thine own, upturn'd – alas, in sorrow!
Was it not Fate, that, on this July midnight –
Was it not Fate, (whose name is also Sorrow,)
That bade me pause before that garden-gate,
To breathe the incense of those slumbering roses?

No footstep stirred: the hated world all slept,
Save only thee and me. (Oh, Heaven! – oh, God!
How my heart beats in coupling those two words!)
Save only thee and me. I paused – I looked –
And in an instant all things disappeared.
(Ah, bear in mind this garden was enchanted!)
The pearly lustre of the moon went out:
The mossy banks and the meandering paths,
The happy flowers and the repining trees,
Were seen no more: the very roses' odors
Died in the arms of the adoring airs.
All – all expired save thee – save less than thou:
Save only the divine light in thine eyes –
Save but the soul in thine uplifted eyes.
I saw but them – they were the world to me.
I saw but them – saw only them for hours –
Saw only them until the moon went down.
What wild heart-histories seemed to lie enwritten
Upon those crystalline, celestial spheres!
How dark a wo! yet how sublime a hope!
How silently serene a sea of pride!
How daring an ambition! yet how deep –
How fathomless a capacity for love!

But now, at length, dear Dian sank from sight,
Into a western couch of thunder-cloud;
And thou, a ghost, amid the entombing trees
Didst glide away. *Only thine eyes remained.*
They *would not* go – they never yet have gone.
Lighting my lonely pathway home that night,
They have not left me (as my hopes have) since.
They follow me – they lead me through the years.
They are my ministers – yet I their slave.
Their office is to illumine and enkindle –
My duty, *to be saved* by their bright light,
And purified in their electric fire,
And sanctified in their elysian fire.
They fill my soul with Beauty (which is Hope,)
And are far up in Heaven – the stars I kneel to
In the sad, silent watches of my night;
While even in the meridian glare of day
I see them still – two sweetly scintillant
Venuses, unextinguished by the sun!

ANNABEL LEE

It was many and many a year ago,
　　In a kingdom by the sea,
That a maiden there lived whom you may know
　　By the name of Annabel Lee; –
And this maiden she lived with no other thought
　　Than to love and be loved by me.

She was a child and *I* was a child,
　　In this kingdom by the sea,
But we loved with a love that was more than love –
　　I and my Annabel Lee –
With a love that the wingéd seraphs of Heaven
　　Coveted her and me.

And this was the reason that, long ago,
　　In this kingdom by the sea,
A wind blew out of a cloud by night
　　Chilling my Annabel Lee;
So that her high-born kinsmen came
　　And bore her away from me,
To shut her up in a sepulchre
　　In this kingdom by the sea.

The angels, not half so happy in Heaven,
　　Went envying her and me;
Yes! that was the reason (as all men know,
　　In this kingdom by the sea)
That the wind came out of the cloud, chilling
　　And killing my Annabel Lee.

But our love it was stronger by far than the love
　　Of those who were older than we –
　　Of many far wiser than we –
And neither the angels in Heaven above
　　Nor the demons down under the sea
Can ever dissever my soul from the soul
　　Of the beautiful Annabel Lee: –

For the moon never beams without bringing me
　　　dreams
　　Of the beautiful Annabel Lee;
And the stars never rise but I see the bright eyes
　　Of the beautiful Annabel Lee;
And so, all the night-tide, I lie down by the side
Of my darling, my darling, my life and my bride
　　In her sepulchre there by the sea –
　　In her tomb by the side of the sea.

LENORE

Ah, broken is the golden bowl! – the spirit flown forever!
Let the bell toll! – a saintly soul floats on the Stygian river: –
And, Guy De Vere, hast *thou* no tear? – weep now or
    never more!
See! on yon drear and rigid bier low lies thy love, Lenore!
Come, let the burial rite be read – the funeral song be sung! –
An anthem for the queenliest dead that ever died so young –
A dirge for her the doubly dead in that she died so young.

"Wretches! ye loved her for her wealth and ye hated her
    for her pride;
And, when she fell in feeble health, ye blessed her –
    that she died: –
How *shall* the ritual then be read – the requiem how be sung
By you – by yours, the evil eye – by yours the slanderous
    tongue
That did to death the innocence that died and died so
    young?"

Peccavimus: – yet rave not thus! but let a Sabbath song
Go up to God so solemnly the dead may feel no wrong!
The sweet Lenore hath gone before, with Hope that
    flew beside,
Leaving thee wild for the dear child that should have
    been thy bride –

For her, the fair and debonair, that now so lowly lies,
The life upon her yellow hair, but not within her eyes –
The life still there upon her hair, the death upon her eyes.

"Avaunt! – avaunt! to friends from fiends the indignant
     ghost is riven –
From Hell unto a high estate within the utmost Heaven –
From moan and groan to a golden throne beside the
     King of Heaven: –
Let *no* bell toll, then, lest her soul, amid its hallowed mirth
Should catch the note as it doth float up from the
     damnéd Earth!
And I – tonight my heart is light: – no dirge will I upraise,
But waft the angel on her flight with a Pæan of old days!"

ELIZABETH

Elizabeth – it surely is most fit
(Logic and common usage so commanding)
In thy own book that *first* thy name be writ,
Zeno[1] and other sages notwithstanding;
And *I* have other reasons for so doing
Besides my innate love of contradiction;
Each poet – *if* a poet – in pursuing
The muses thro' their bowers of Truth or Fiction,
Has studied very little of his part,
Read nothing, written less – in short's a fool
Endued with neither soul, nor sense, nor art,
Being ignorant of one important rule,
Employed in even the theses of the school –
Called – I forget the heathenish Greek name –
(Called any thing, its meaning is the same)
"Always write *first* things uppermost in the heart."

1 It was a saying of this philosopher "that one's
own name should never appear in one's own book."

EULALIE – A SONG

I dwelt alone
In a world of moan,
And my soul was a stagnant tide,
Till the fair and gentle Eulalie became my blushing
bride –
Till the yellow-haired young Eulalie became my
smiling bride.

Ah, less – less bright
The stars of the night
Than the eyes of the radiant girl!
And never a flake
That the vapor can make
With the moon-tints of purple and pearl,
Can vie with the modest Eulalie's most unregarded
curl –
Can compare with the bright-eyed Eulalie's most
humble and careless curl.

Now Doubt – now Pain
Come never again,
For her soul gives me sigh for sigh,
And all day long
Shines, bright and strong,
Astarté within the sky,
While ever to her dear Eulalie upturns her matron eye –
While ever to her young Eulalie upturns her violet eye.

TO MARGARET

Who hath seduced thee to this foul revolt   Milton Par. Lost Bk. I
From the pure well of Beauty undefiled?   Somebody
So banished from true wisdom to prefer
Such squalid wit to honourable rhyme?   Cowper's Task, Book I
To write? To scribble? Nonsense and no
     more?   Shakespeare
I will not write upon this argument   do. Troilus & Cressida
To write is human – not to write divine.   Pope Essay on Man

"TO OCTAVIA"

When wit, and wine, and friends have met
And laughter crowns the festive hour
In vain I struggle to forget
Still does my heart confess thy power
    And fondly turn to thee!
But Octavia, do not strive to rob
My heart, of all that soothes its pain
The mournful hope that every throb
    Will make it break for thee!

SONNET – TO ZANTE

Fair isle, that from the fairest of all flowers,
    Thy gentlest of all gentle names dost take!
How many memories of what radiant hours
    At sight of thee and thine at once awake!
How many scenes of what departed bliss!
    How many thoughts of what entombéd hopes!
How many visions of a maiden that is
    No more – no more upon thy verdant slopes!
No more! alas, that magical sad sound
    Transforming all! Thy charms shall please *no more* –
Thy memory *no more!* Accurséd ground
    Henceforth I hold thy flower-enamelled shore,
O hyacinthine isle! O purple Zante!
    "Isola d'oro! Fior di Levante!"

TO MISS LOUISE OLIVIA HUNTER

Though I turn, I fly not —
   I cannot depart;
I would try, but try not
   To release my heart.
And my hopes are dying
While, on dreams relying,
   I am spelled by art.

Thus the bright snake coiling
   'Neath the forest tree
Wins the bird, beguiling
   To come down and see:
Like that bird the lover
Round his fate will hover
Till the blow is over
   And he sinks — like me.

FOR ANNIE

Thank Heaven! the crisis —
    The danger is past,
And the lingering illness
    Is over at last —
And the fever called "Living"
    Is conquered at last.

Sadly, I know
    I am shorn of my strength,
And no muscle I move
    As I lie at full length —
But no matter! — I feel
    I am better at length.

And I rest so composedly,
    Now, in my bed,
That any beholder
    Might fancy me dead —
Might start at beholding me,
    Thinking me dead.

The moaning and groaning,
  The sighing and sobbing,
Are quieted now,
  With that horrible throbbing
At heart: – ah, that horrible,
  Horrible throbbing!

The sickness – the nausea –
  The pitiless pain –
Have ceased, with the fever
  That maddened my brain –
With the fever called "Living"
  That burned in my brain.

And oh! of all tortures
  That torture the worst
Has abated – the terrible
  Torture of thirst
For the napthaline river
  Of Passion accurst: –
I have drank of a water
  That quenches all thirst: –

Of a water that flows,
    With a lullaby sound,
From a spring but a very few
    Feet under ground —
From a cavern not very far
    Down under ground.

And ah! let it never
    Be foolishly said
That my room it is gloomy
    And narrow my bed;
For man never slept
    In a different bed —
And, to *sleep*, you must slumber
    In just such a bed.

My tantalized spirit
    Here blandly reposes,
Forgetting, or never
    Regretting its roses —
Its old agitations
    Of myrtles and roses:

For now, while so quietly
    Lying, it fancies
A holier odor
    About it, of pansies —
A rosemary odor,
    Commingled with pansies —
With rue and the beautiful
    Puritan pansies.

And so it lies happily,
    Bathing in many
A dream of the truth
    And the beauty of Annie —
Drowned in a bath
    Of the tresses of Annie.

She tenderly kissed me,
    She fondly caressed,
And then I fell gently
    To sleep on her breast —
Deeply to sleep
    From the heaven of her breast.

When the light was extinguished,
  She covered me warm,
And she prayed to the angels
  To keep me from harm –
To the queen of the angels
  To shield me from harm.

And I lie so composedly,
  Now, in my bed,
(Knowing her love)
  That you fancy me dead –
And I rest so contentedly,
  Now in my bed,
(With her love at my breast)
  That you fancy me dead –
That you shudder to look at me,
  Thinking me dead: –

But my heart it is brighter
  Than all of the many
Stars in the sky,
  For it sparkles with Annie –
It glows with the light
  Of the love of my Annie –
With the thought of the light
  Of the eyes of my Annie.

TO M. L. S ——

Of all who hail thy presence as the morning –
Of all to whom thine absence is the night –
The blotting utterly from out high heaven
The sacred sun – of all who, weeping, bless thee
Hourly for hope – for life – ah! above all,
For the resurrection of deep-buried faith
In Truth – in Virtue – in Humanity –
Of all who, on Despair's unhallowed bed
Lying down to die, have suddenly arisen
At thy soft-murmured words, "Let there be light!"
At the soft-murmured words that were fulfilled
In the seraphic glancing of thine eyes –
Of all who owe thee most – whose gratitude
Nearest resembles worship – oh, remember
The truest – the most fervently devoted,
And think that these weak lines are written by him –
By him who, as he pens them, thrills to think
His spirit is communing with an angel's.

TO —— —— ——

Not long ago, the writer of these lines,
In the mad pride of intellectuality,
Maintained "the power of words" – denied that ever
A thought arose within the human brain
Beyond the utterance of the human tongue;
And now, as if in mockery of that boast,
Two words – two foreign soft dissyllables –
Italian tones made only to be murmured
By angels dreaming in the moonlit "dew
That hangs like chains of pearl on Hermon hill" –
Have stirred from out the abysses of his heart,
Unthought-like thoughts that are the souls of thought,
Richer, far wilder, far diviner visions
Than even the seraph harper, Israfel,
Who has "the sweetest voice of all God's creatures,"
Could hope to utter. And I! my spells are broken.
The pen falls powerless from my shivering hand.

With thy dear name as text, though bidden by thee,
I cannot write – I cannot speak or think,
Alas, I cannot feel; for 'tis not feeling,
This standing motionless upon the golden
Threshold of the wide-open gate of dreams,
Gazing, entranced, adown the gorgeous vista,
And thrilling as I see upon the right,
Upon the left, and all the way along
Amid empurpled vapors, far away
To where the prospect terminates – *thee only*.

A VALENTINE TO —— —— ——

For her this rhyme is penned, whose luminous eyes,
  Brightly expressive as the twins of Lœda,
Shall find her own sweet name, that, nestling lies
  Upon the page, enwrapped from every reader.
Search narrowly the lines! – they hold a treasure
  Divine – a talisman – an amulet
That must be worn *at heart*. Search well the measure –
  The words – the syllables! Do not forget
The trivialest point, or you may lose your labor!
  And yet there is in this no Gordian knot
Which one might not undo without a sabre,
  If one could merely comprehend the plot.
Enwritten upon the leaf where now are peering
  Eyes scintillating soul, there lie *perdus*
Three eloquent words oft uttered in the hearing
  Of poets, by poets – as the name is a poet's, too.
Its letters, although naturally lying
  Like the knight Pinto – Mendez Ferdinando –
Still form a synonym for Truth. – Cease trying!
  You will not read the riddle, though you do the best
    you *can* do.

TO ——

The bowers whereat, in dreams, I see
    The wantonest singing birds,
Are lips – and all thy melody
    Of lip-begotten words –

Thine eyes, in Heaven of heart enshrined
    Then desolately fall,
O God! on my funereal mind
    Like starlight on a pall –

Thy heart – *thy* heart! – I wake and sigh,
    And sleep to dream till day
Of the truth that gold can never buy –
    Of the baubles that it may.

BRIDAL BALLAD

The ring is on my hand,
    And the wreath is on my brow;
Satins and jewels grand
Are all at my command,
    And I am happy now.

And my lord he loves me well;
    But, when first he breathed his vow,
I felt my bosom swell —
For the words rang as a knell,
And the voice seemed *his* who fell
In the battle down the dell,
    And who is happy now.

But he spoke to re-assure me,
    And he kissed my pallid brow,
While a reverie came o'er me,
And to the church-yard bore me,
And I sighed to him before me,
(Thinking him dead D'Elormie,)
    "Oh, I am happy now!"

And thus the words were spoken;
    And this the plighted vow;
And, though my faith be broken,
And, though my heart be broken,
Here is a ring, as token
    That I am happy now! –
Behold the golden token
    That *proves* me happy now!

Would God I could awaken!
    For I dream I know not how,
And my soul is sorely shaken
Lest an evil step be taken, –
Lest the dead who is forsaken
    May not be happy now.

SONG

I saw thee on thy bridal day –
   When a burning blush came o'er thee,
Though happiness around thee lay,
   The world all love before thee:

And in thine eye a kindling light
   (Whatever it might be)
Was all on Earth my aching sight
   Of Loveliness could see.

That blush, perhaps, was maiden shame –
   As such it well may pass –
Though its glow hath raised a fiercer flame
   In the breast of him, alas!

Who saw thee on that bridal day,
   When that deep blush *would* come o'er thee,
Though happiness around thee lay,
   The world all love before thee.

TO THE RIVER ——

Fair river! in thy bright, clear flow
    Of crystal, wandering water,
Thou art an emblem of the glow
        Of beauty – the unhidden heart –
        The playful maziness of art
    In old Alberto's daughter;

But when within thy wave she looks –
    Which glistens then, and trembles –
Why, then, the prettiest of brooks
    Her worshipper resembles;
For in his heart, as in thy stream,
    Her image deeply lies –
His heart which trembles at the beam
    Of her soul-searching eyes.

SPIRITS OF THE DEAD

I

Thy soul shall find itself alone
'Mid dark thoughts of the gray tomb-stone –
Not one, of all the crowd, to pry
Into thine hour of secrecy:

II

Be silent in that solitude,
    Which is not loneliness – for then
The spirits of the dead who stood
    In life before thee are again
In death around thee – and their will
Shall overshadow thee: be still.

III

The night – tho' clear – shall frown –
And the stars shall look not down,
From their high thrones in the heaven,
With light like Hope to mortals given –
But their red orbs, without beam,
To thy weariness shall seem
As a burning and a fever
Which would cling to thee for ever.

IV

Now are thoughts thou shalt not banish –
Now are visions ne'er to vanish –
From thy spirit shall they pass
No more – like dew-drop from the grass.

V

The breeze – the breath of God – is still –
And the mist upon the hill
Shadowy – shadowy – yet unbroken,
Is a symbol and a token –
How it hangs upon the trees,
A mystery of mysteries! –

EVENING STAR

'Twas noontide of summer,
    And mid-time of night;
And stars, in their orbits,
    Shone pale, thro' the light
Of the brighter, cold moon,
    'Mid planets her slaves,
Herself in the Heavens,
    Her beam on the waves.
    I gaz'd awhile
    On her cold smile;
Too cold – too cold for me –
    There pass'd, as a shroud,
    A fleecy cloud,
And I turn'd away to thee,
    Proud Evening Star,
    In thy glory afar,
And dearer thy beam shall be;
    For joy to my heart
    Is the proud part
Thou bearest in Heav'n at night,
    And more I admire
    Thy distant fire,
Than that colder, lowly light.

IMITATION

A dark unfathom'd tide
Of interminable pride –
A mystery, and a dream,
Should my early life seem;
I say that dream was fraught
With a wild, and waking thought
Of beings that have been,
Which my spirit hath not seen,
Had I let them pass me by,
With a dreaming eye!
Let none of earth inherit
That vision on my spirit;
Those thoughts I would controul,
As a spell upon his soul:
For that bright hope at last
And that light time have past,
And my worldly rest hath gone
With a sight as it pass'd on:
I care not tho' it perish
With a thought I then did cherish.

"STANZAS"

How often we forget all time, when lone
Admiring Nature's universal throne;
Her woods – her wilds – her mountains – the intense
Reply of HERS to OUR intelligence!

1

In youth have I known one with whom the Earth
In secret communing held – as he with it,
In day light, and in beauty from his birth:
Whose fervid, flick'ring torch of life was lit
From the sun and stars, whence he had drawn forth
A passionate light – such for his spirit was fit –
And yet that spirit knew – not in the hour
Of its own fervor – what had o'er it power.

2

Perhaps it may be that my mind is wrought
To a fervor by the moon beam that hangs o'er,
But I will half believe that wild light fraught
With more of sov'reignty than ancient lore
Hath ever told – or is it of a thought
The unembodied essence, and no more
That with a quick'ning spell doth o'er us pass
As dew of the night-time, o'er the summer grass?

3

Doth o'er us pass, when, as th' expanding eye
To the lov'd object — so the tear to the lid
Will start, which lately slept in apathy?
And yet it need not be — (that object) hid
From us in life — but common — which doth lie
Each hour before us — but *then* only bid
With a strange sound, as of a harp-string broken
T' awake us — 'Tis a symbol and a token.

4

Of what in other worlds shall be — and giv'n
In beauty by our God, to those alone
Who otherwise would fall from life and Heav'n
Drawn by their heart's passion, and that tone,
That high tone of the spirit which hath striv'n
Tho' not with Faith — with godliness — whose throne
With desp'rate energy 't hath beaten down;
Wearing its own deep feeling as a crown.

DREAMS

Oh! that my young life were a lasting dream!
My spirit not awak'ning till the beam
Of an Eternity should bring the morrow:
Yes! tho' that long dream were of hopeless sorrow,
'Twere better than the dull reality
Of waking life to him whose heart shall be,
And hath been ever, on the chilly earth,
A chaos of deep passion from his birth!

But should it be – that dream eternally
Continuing – as dreams have been to me
In my young boyhood – should it thus be given,
'Twere folly still to hope for higher Heaven!
For I have revell'd, when the sun was bright
In the summer sky; in dreamy fields of light,
And left unheedingly my very heart
In climes of mine imagining – apart
From mine own home, with beings that have been
Of mine own thought – what more could I have seen?

'Twas once and *only* once and the wild hour
From my remembrance shall not pass – some power
Or spell had bound me – 'twas the chilly wind
Came o'er me in the night and left behind
Its image on my spirit, or the moon
Shone on my slumbers in her lofty noon
Too coldly – or the stars – howe'er it was
That dream was as that night wind – let it pass.

I have been happy – tho' but in a dream.
I have been happy – and I love the theme –
Dreams! in their vivid colouring of life –
As in that fleeting, shadowy, misty strife
Of semblance with reality which brings
To the delirious eye more lovely things
Of Paradise and Love – and all our own!
Than young Hope in his sunniest hour hath known.

A DREAM

In visions of the dark night
    I have dreamed of joy departed –
But a waking dream of life and light
    Hath left me broken-hearted.

Ah! what is not a dream by day
    To him whose eyes are cast
On things around him with a ray
    Turned back upon the past?

That holy dream – that holy dream,
    While all the world were chiding,
Hath cheered me as a lovely beam
    A lonely spirit guiding.

What though that light, thro' storm and night,
    So trembled from afar –
What could there be more purely bright
    In Truth's day-star?

DREAM-LAND

By a route obscure and lonely,
Haunted by ill angels only,
Where an Eidolon, named NIGHT,
On a black throne reigns upright,
I have reached these lands but newly
From an ultimate dim Thule –
From a wild weird clime that lieth, sublime,
    Out of SPACE – out of TIME.

Bottomless vales and boundless floods,
And chasms, and caves, and Titan woods,
With forms that no man can discover
For the tears that drip all over;
Mountains toppling evermore
Into seas without a shore;
Seas that restlessly aspire,
Surging, unto skies of fire;
Lakes that endlessly outspread
Their lone waters – lone and dead, –
Their still waters – still and chilly
With the snows of the lolling lily.

By the lakes that thus outspread
Their lone waters, lone and dead, –
Their sad waters, sad and chilly
With the snows of the lolling lily, –
By the mountains – near the river
Murmuring lowly, murmuring ever, –
By the grey woods, – by the swamp
Where the toad and the newt encamp, –
By the dismal tarns and pools
   Where dwell the Ghouls, –
By each spot the most unholy –
In each nook most melancholy, –
There the traveller meets, aghast,
Sheeted Memories of the Past –
Shrouded forms that start and sigh
As they pass the wanderer by –
White-robed forms of friends long given,
In agony, to the Earth – and Heaven.

For the heart whose woes are legion
'Tis a peaceful, soothing region –
For the spirit that walks in shadow
'Tis – oh 'tis an Eldorado!
But the traveller, travelling through it,
May not – dare not openly view it;
Never its mysteries are exposed
To the weak human eye unclosed;

So wills its King, who hath forbid
The uplifting of the fringéd lid;
And thus the sad Soul that here passes
Beholds it but through darkened glasses.

By a route obscure and lonely,
Haunted by ill angels only,
Where an Eidolon, named NIGHT,
On a black throne reigns upright,
I have wandered home but newly
From this ultimate dim Thule.

A DREAM WITHIN A DREAM

Take this kiss upon the brow!
And, in parting from you now,
Thus much let me avow –
You are not wrong, who deem
That my days have been a dream;
Yet if Hope has flown away
In a night, or in a day,
In a vision, or in none,
Is it therefore the less *gone*?
All that we see or seem
Is but a dream within a dream.

I stand amid the roar
Of a surf-tormented shore,
And I hold within my hand
Grains of the golden sand –
How few! yet how they creep
Through my fingers to the deep,
While I weep – while I weep!
O God! can I not grasp
Them with a tighter clasp?
O God! can I not save
One from the pitiless wave?
Is *all* that we see or seem
But a dream within a dream?

FAIRY LAND

Sit down beside me, Isabel,
Here, dearest, where the moonbeam fell
Just now so fairy-like and well.
Now thou art dress'd for paradise!
I am star-stricken with thine eyes!
My soul is lolling on thy sighs!
Thy hair is lifted by the moon
Like flowers by the low breath of June!
Sit down, sit down – how came we here?
Or is it all but a dream, my dear?

You know that most enormous flower –
That rose – that what d' ye call it – that hung
Up like a dog-star in this bower –
To-day (the wind blew, and) it swung
So impudently in my face,
So like a thing alive you know,
I tore it from its pride of place
And shook it into pieces – so
Be all ingratitude requited.
The winds ran off with it delighted,
And, thro' the opening left, as soon
As she threw off her cloak, yon moon
Has sent a ray down with a tune.
And this ray is a *fairy* ray –

Did you not say so, Isabel?
How fantastically it fell
With a spiral twist and a swell,
And over the wet grass rippled away
With a tinkling like a bell!
In my own country all the way
We can discover a moon ray
Which thro' some tatter'd curtain pries
Into the darkness of a room,
Is by (the very source of gloom)
The motes, and dust, and flies,
On which it trembles and lies
Like joy upon sorrow!
O, *when* will come the morrow?
Isabel! do you not fear
The night and the wonders here?
Dim vales! and shadowy floods!
And cloudy-looking woods
Whose forms we can't discover
For the tears that drip all over!

Huge moons – see? wax and wane
Again – again – again –
Every moment of the night –
Forever changing places!
How they put out the starlight
With the breath from their pale faces!

Lo! one is coming down
With its centre on the crown
Of a mountain's eminence!
Down – still down – and down –
Now deep shall be – O deep!
The passion of our sleep!
For that wide circumference
In easy drapery falls
Drowsily over halls –
Over ruin'd walls –
Over waterfalls,
(Silent waterfalls!)
O'er the strange woods – o'er the sea –
Alas! over the sea!

FAIRY-LAND

Dim vales – and shadowy floods –
And cloudy-looking woods,
Whose forms we can't discover
For the tears that drip all over
Huge moons there wax and wane –
Again – again – again –
Every moment of the night –
Forever changing places –
And they put out the star-light
With the breath from their pale faces.
About twelve by the moon-dial
One more filmy than the rest
(A kind which, upon trial,
They have found to be the best)
Comes down – still down – and down
With its centre on the crown
Of a mountain's eminence,
While its wide circumference
In easy drapery falls
Over hamlets, over halls,
Wherever they may be –
O'er the strange woods – o'er the sea –
Over spirits on the wing –
Over every drowsy thing –
And buries them up quite

In a labyrinth of light —
And then, how deep! — O, deep!
Is the passion of their sleep.
In the morning they arise,
And their moony covering
Is soaring in the skies,
With the tempests as they toss,
Like —— almost any thing —
Or a yellow Albatross.
They use that moon no more
For the same end as before —
Videlicet a tent —
Which I think extravagant:
Its atomies, however,
Into a shower dissever,
Of which those butterflies,
Of Earth, who seek the skies,
And so come down again
(Never-contented things!)
Have brought a specimen
Upon their quivering wings.

"ALONE"

From childhood's hour I have not been
As others were – I have not seen
As others saw – I could not bring
My passions from a common spring –
From the same source I have not taken
My sorrow – I could not awaken
My heart to joy at the same tone –
And all I lov'd – *I* lov'd alone –
Then – in my childhood – in the dawn
Of a most stormy life – was drawn
From ev'ry depth of good and ill
The mystery which binds me still –
From the torrent, or the fountain –
From the red cliff of the mountain –
From the sun that 'round me roll'd
In its autumn tint of gold –
From the lightning in the sky
As it pass'd me flying by –
From the thunder, and the storm –
And the cloud that took the form
(When the rest of Heaven was blue)
Of a demon in my view –

"TO ISAAC LEA"

It was my choice or chance or curse
To adopt the cause for better or worse
And with my worldly goods and wit
And soul and body worship it.

TO ——

I heed not that my earthly lot
    Hath – little of Earth in it –
That years of love have been forgot
    In the hatred of a minute: –
I mourn not that the desolate
    Are happier, sweet, than I,
But that *you* sorrow for *my* fate
    Who am a passer by.

AN ACROSTIC

Elizabeth it is in vain you say
"Love not" – thou sayest it in so sweet a way:
In vain those words from thee or L. E. L.
Zantippe's talents had enforced so well:
Ah! if that language from thy heart arise,
Breathe it less gently forth – and veil thine eyes.
Endymion, recollect, when Luna tried
To cure his love – was cured of all beside –
His folly – pride – and passion – for he died.

SONNET – SILENCE

There are some qualities – some incorporate things,
   That have a double life, which thus is made
A type of that twin entity which springs
   From matter and light, evinced in solid and shade.
There is a two-fold *Silence* – sea and shore –
   Body and soul. One dwells in lonely places,
   Newly with grass o'ergrown; some solemn graces,
Some human memories and tearful lore,
Render him terrorless: his name's "No More."
He is the corporate Silence: dread him not!
   No power hath he of evil in himself;
But should some urgent fate (untimely lot!)
   Bring thee to meet his shadow (nameless elf,
That haunteth the lone regions where hath trod
No foot of man,) commend thyself to God!

"MYSTERIOUS STAR!"

Mysterious star!
Thou wert my dream
All a long summer night –
Be now my theme!
By this clear stream,
Of thee will I write;
Meantime from afar
Bathe me in light!

Thy world has not the dross of ours,
Yet all the beauty – all the flowers
That list our love, or deck our bowers
In dreamy gardens, where do lie
Dreamy maidens all the day,
While the silver winds of Circassy
On violet couches faint away.

Little – oh! little dwells in thee
Like unto what on earth we see:
Beauty's eye is here the bluest
In the falsest and untruest –
On the sweetest air doth float
The most sad and solemn note –
If with thee be broken hearts,
Joy so peacefully departs,
That its echo still doth dwell,
Like the murmur in the shell.
Thou! thy truest type of grief
Is the gently falling leaf –
Thou! thy framing is so holy
Sorrow is not melancholy.

"THE HAPPIEST DAY"

The happiest day – the happiest hour
   My sear'd and blighted heart hath known,
The highest hope of pride, and power,
   I feel hath flown.

Of power! said I? yes! such I ween
   But they have vanish'd long alas!
The visions of my youth have been –
   But let them pass.

And, pride, what have I now with thee?
   Another brow may ev'n inherit
The venom thou hast pour'd on me –
   Be still my spirit.

The happiest day – the happiest hour
    Mine eyes shall see – have ever seen
The brightest glance of pride and power
    I feel – have been:

But were that hope of pride and power
    Now offer'd, with the pain
Ev'n *then* I felt – that brightest hour
    I would not live again:

For on its wing was dark alloy
    And as it flutter'd – fell
An essence – powerful to destroy
    A soul that knew it well.

THE LAKE ── TO──

In spring of youth it was my lot
To haunt of the wide world a spot
The which I could not love the less –
So lovely was the loneliness
Of a wild lake, with black rock bound,
And the tall pines that towered around.

But when the Night had thrown her pall
Upon that spot, as upon all,
And the mystic wind went by
Murmuring in melody –
Then – ah then I would awake
To the terror of the lone lake.

Yet that terror was not fright,
But a tremulous delight –
A feeling not the jewelled mine
Could teach or bribe me to define –
Nor Love – although the Love were thine.

Death was in that poisonous wave,
And in its gulf a fitting grave
For him who thence could solace bring
To his lone imagining –
Whose solitary soul could make
An Eden of that dim lake.

"LINES ON JOE LOCKE"

As for Locke, he is all in my eye,
    May the d——l right soon for his soul call.
He never was known to lie –
    In bed at a *reveillé* "roll call."

John Locke was a notable name;
    Joe Locke is a greater; in short,
The former was well known to fame,
    But the latter's well known "to report."

TO F——S S. O——D

Thou wouldst be loved? – then let thy heart
    From its present pathway part not!
Being everything which now thou art,
    Be nothing which thou art not.
So with the world thy gentle ways,
    Thy grace, thy more than beauty,
Shall be an endless theme of praise,
    And love – a simple duty.

TO F——

Beloved! amid the earnest woes
    That crowd around my earthly path –
(Drear path, alas! where grows
Not even one lonely rose) –
    My soul at least a solace hath
In dreams of thee, and therein knows
An Eden of bland repose.

And thus thy memory is to me
    Like some enchanted far-off isle
In some tumultuous sea –
Some ocean throbbing far and free
    With storms – but where meanwhile
Serenest skies continually
    Just o'er that one bright island smile.

ISRAFEL[1]

In Heaven a spirit doth dwell
    "Whose heart-strings are a lute;"
None sing so wildly well
As the angel Israfel,
And the giddy stars (so legends tell)
Ceasing their hymns, attend the spell
    Of his voice, all mute.

Tottering above
    In her highest noon,
    The enamoured moon
Blushes with love,
    While, to listen, the red levin
    (With the rapid Pleiads, even,
    Which were seven,)
    Pauses in Heaven.

And they say (the starry choir
    And the other listening things)
That Israfeli's fire
Is owing to that lyre
    By which he sits and sings –
The trembling living wire
Of those unusual strings.

But the skies that angel trod,
    Where deep thoughts are a duty –
Where Love's a grown-up God –
    Where the Houri glances are
Imbued with all the beauty
    Which we worship in a star.

Therefore, thou art not wrong,
    Israfeli, who despisest
An unimpassioned song;
To thee the laurels belong,
    Best bard, because the wisest!
Merrily live, and long!

The ecstasies above
    With thy burning measures suit –
Thy grief, thy joy, thy hate, thy love,
With the fervour of thy lute –
Well may the stars be mute!

Yes, Heaven is thine; but this
    Is a world of sweets and sours;
    Our flowers are merely – flowers,
And the shadow of thy perfect bliss
    Is the sunshine of ours.

If I could dwell
Where Israfel
   Hath dwelt, and he where I,
He might not sing so wildly well
   A mortal melody,
While a bolder note than this might swell
   From my lyre within the sky.

---

1 And the angel Israfel, whose heart-strings are a lute, and who has the sweetest voice of all God's creatures. — KORAN

TO ONE IN PARADISE

Thou wast that all to me, love,
   For which my soul did pine –
A green isle in the sea, love,
   A fountain and a shrine,
All wreathed with fairy fruits and flowers,
   And all the flowers were mine.

Ah, dream too bright to last!
   Ah, starry Hope! that didst arise
But to be overcast!
   A voice from out the Future cries,
"On! on!" – but o'er the Past
   (Dim gulf!) my spirit hovering lies
Mute, motionless, aghast!

For, alas! alas! with me
   The light of Life is o'er!
No more – no more – no more –
(Such language holds the solemn sea
   To the sands upon the shore)
Shall bloom the thunder-blasted tree,
   Or the stricken eagle soar!

And all my days are trances,
    And all my nightly dreams
Are where thy grey eye glances,
    And where thy footstep gleams –
In what ethereal dances,
By what eternal streams.

"DEEP IN EARTH"

Deep in earth my love is lying
    And I must weep alone.

THE CONQUEROR WORM

Lo! 'tis a gala night
    Within the lonesome latter years!
An angel throng, bewinged, bedight
    In veils, and drowned in tears,
Sit in a theatre, to see
    A play of hopes and fears,
While the orchestra breathes fitfully
    The music of the spheres.

Mimes, in the form of God on high,
    Mutter and mumble low,
And hither and thither fly –
    Mere puppets they, who come and go
At bidding of vast formless things
    That shift the scenery to and fro,
Flapping from out their Condor wings
    Invisible Wo!

That motley drama – oh, be sure
    It shall not be forgot!
With its Phantom chased for evermore,
    By a crowd that seize it not,

Through a circle that ever returneth in
  To the self-same spot,
And much of Madness, and more of Sin,
  And Horror the soul of the plot.

But see, amid the mimic rout
  A crawling shape intrude!
A blood-red thing that writhes from out
  The scenic solitude!
It writhes! — it writhes! — with mortal pangs
  The mimes become its food,
And seraphs sob at vermin fangs
  In human gore imbued.

Out — out are the lights — out all!
  And, over each quivering form,
The curtain, a funeral pall,
  Comes down with the rush of a storm,
While the angels, all pallid and wan,
  Uprising, unveiling, affirm
That the play is the tragedy, "Man,"
  And its hero the Conqueror Worm.

HYMN

At morn – at noon – at twilight dim –
Maria! thou hast heard my hymn!
In joy and wo – in good and ill –
Mother of God, be with me still!
When the Hours flew brightly by,
And not a cloud obscured the sky,
My soul, lest it should truant be,
Thy grace did guide to thine and thee;
Now, when storms of Fate o'ercast
Darkly my Present and my Past,
Let my Future radiant shine
With sweet hopes of thee and thine!

ENIGMA

The noblest name in Allegory's page,
The hand that traced inexorable rage;
A pleasing moralist whose page refined,
Displays the deepest knowledge of the mind;
A tender poet of a foreign tongue,
(Indited in the language that he sung.)
A bard of brilliant but unlicensed page
At once the shame and glory of our age,
The prince of harmony and stirling sense,
An ancient dramatist of eminence,
The bard that paints imagination's powers,
And him whose song revives departed hours,
Once more an ancient tragic bard recall,
In boldness of design surpassing all.
These names when rightly read, a name known
Which gathers all their glories in its own.

SERENADE

So sweet the hour – so calm the time,
I feel it more than half a crime
When Nature sleeps and stars are mute,
To mar the silence ev'n with lute.
At rest on ocean's brilliant dies
An image of Elysium lies:
Seven Pleiades entranced in Heaven,
Form in the deep another seven:
Endymion nodding from above
Sees in the sea a second love:
Within the valleys dim and brown,
And on the spectral mountains' crown
The wearied light is lying down:
And earth, and stars, and sea, and sky
Are redolent of sleep, as I
Am redolent of thee and thine
Enthralling love, my Adeline.
But list, O list! – so soft and low
Thy lover's voice to night shall flow
That, scarce awake, thy soul shall deem
My words the music of a dream.
Thus, while no single sound too rude,
Upon thy slumber shall intrude,
Our thoughts, our souls – O God above!
In every deed shall mingle, love.

THE COLISEUM

Type of the antique Rome! Rich reliquary
Of lofty contemplation left to Time
By buried centuries of pomp and power!
At length – at length – after so many days
Of weary pilgrimage and burning thirst,
(Thirst for the springs of lore that in thee lie,)
I kneel, an altered and an humble man,
Amid thy shadows, and so drink within
My very soul thy grandeur, gloom, and glory!

Vastness! and Age! and Memories of Eld!
Silence! and Desolation! and dim Night!
I feel ye now – I feel ye in your strength –
O spells more sure than e'er Judæan king
Taught in the gardens of Gethsemane!
O charms more potent than the rapt Chaldee
Ever drew down from out the quiet stars!

Here, where a hero fell, a column falls!
Here, where the mimic eagle glared in gold,
A midnight vigil holds the swarthy bat!
Here, where the dames of Rome their gilded hair
Waved to the wind, now wave the reed and thistle!
Here, where on golden throne the monarch lolled,
Glides, spectre-like, unto his marble home,

Lit by the wan light of the horned moon,
The swift and silent lizard of the stones!

But stay! these walls – these ivy-clad arcades –
These mouldering plinths – these sad and blackened
    shafts –
These vague entablatures – this crumbling frieze –
These shattered cornices – this wreck – this ruin –
These stones – alas! these gray stones – are they all –
All of the famed, and the colossal left
By the corrosive Hours to Fate and me?

"Not all" – the Echoes answer me – "not all!
"Prophetic sounds and loud, arise forever
"From us, and from all Ruin, unto the wise,
"As melody from Memnon to the Sun.
"We rule the hearts of mightiest men – we rule
"With a despotic sway all giant minds.
"We are not impotent – we pallid stones.
"Not all our power is gone – not all our fame –
"Not all the magic of our high renown –
"Not all the wonder that encircles us –
"Not all the mysteries that in us lie –
"Not all the memories that hang upon
"And cling around about us as a garment,
"Clothing us in a robe of more than glory."

O, TEMPORA! O, MORES!

O, Times! O, Manners! It is my opinion
That you are changing sadly your dominion —
I mean the reign of manners hath long ceased,
For men have none at all, or bad at least;
And as for times, altho' 'tis said by many
The "good old times" were far the worst of any,
Of which sound doctrine I believe each tittle,
Yet still I think these worse than them a little.

I've been a thinking — isn't that the phrase? —
I like your Yankee words and Yankee ways —
I've been a thinking, whether it were best
To take things seriously, or all in jest;
Whether, with grim Heraclitus of yore,
To weep, as he did, till his eyes were sore;
Or rather laugh with him, that queer philosopher,
Democritus of Thrace, who used to toss over
The page of life and grin at the dog-ears,
As though he'd say, "Why, who the devil cares?"

This is a question which, oh heaven, withdraw
The luckless query from a member's claw!
Instead of two sides, Job has nearly eight,
Each fit to furnish forth four hours debate.
What shall be done? I'll lay it on the table,

And take the matter up when I'm more able;
And, in the meantime, to prevent all bother,
I'll neither laugh with one, nor cry with t'other,
Nor deal in flatt'ry or aspersions foul,
But, taking one by each hand, merely growl.

Ah, growl, say you, my friend, and pray at what?
Why, really, sir, I almost had forgot –
But, damn it, sir, I deem it a disgrace
That things should stare us boldly in the face,
And daily strut the street with bows and scrapes,
Who would be men by imitating apes.
I beg your pardon, reader, for the oath
The monkeys make me swear, though something loth;
I'm apt to be discursive in my style,
But pray be patient; yet a little while
Will change me, and as politicians do,
I'll mend my manners and my measures too.

Of all the cities – and I've seen no few;
For I have travelled, friend, as well as you –
I don't remember one, upon my soul,
But take it generally upon the whole,
(As members say they like their logick taken,
Because divided, it may chance be shaken)
So pat, agreeable and vastly proper
As this for a neat, frisky counter-hopper;

Here he may revel to his heart's content,
Flounce like a fish in his own element,
Toss back his fine curls from their forehead fair,
And hop o'er counters with a Vester's air,
Complete at night what he began A.M.,
And having cheated ladies, dance with them;
For, at a ball, what fair one can escape
The pretty little hand that sold her tape,
Or who so cold, so callous to refuse
The youth who cut the ribbon for her shoes!

One of these fish, *par excellence* the beau –
God help me! – it has been my lot to know,
At least by sight, for I'm a timid man,
And always keep from laughing, if I can;
But speak to him, he'll make you such grimace,
Lord! to be grave exceeds the power of face.
The hearts of all the ladies are with him,
Their bright eyes on his Tom and Jerry brim
And dove-tailed coat, obtained at cost; while then
Those eyes won't turn on anything like men.

His very voice is musical delight,
His form, once seen, becomes a part of sight;
In short, his shirt collar, his look, his tone is
The "beau ideal" fancied for Adonis.
Philosophers have often held dispute

As to the seat of thought in man and brute;
For that the power of thought attends the latter
My friend, the beau, hath made a settled matter,
And spite of all dogmas, current in all ages,
One settled fact is better than ten sages.

For he does think, though I am oft in doubt
If I can tell exactly what about.
Ah, yes! his little foot and ankle trim,
'Tis there the seat of reason lies in him,
A wise philosopher would shake his head,
He then, of course, must shake his foot instead.
At me, in vengeance, shall that foot be shaken –
Another proof of thought, I'm not mistaken –
Because to his cat's eyes I hold a glass,
And let him see himself, a proper ass!
I think he'll take this likeness to himself,
But if he won't, *he shall*, a stupid elf,
And, lest the guessing throw the fool in fits,
I close the portrait with the name of PITTS.

SONNET – TO SCIENCE[1]

Science! true daughter of Old Time thou art!
    Who alterest all things with thy peering eyes.
Why preyest thou thus upon the poet's heart,
    Vulture, whose wings are dull realities?
How should he love thee! or how deem thee wise,
    Who wouldst not leave him in his wandering
To seek for treasure in the jewelled skies,
    Albeit he soared with an undaunted wing?
Hast thou not dragged Diana from her car?
    And driven the Hamadryad from the wood
To seek a shelter in some happier star?
    Hast thou not torn the Naiad from her flood,
The Elfin from the green grass, and from me
The summer dream beneath the tamarind tree?

---

1 Private reasons – some of which have reference to the
sin of plagiarism, and others to the date of Tennyson's first
poems – have induced me, after some hesitation, to re-publish
these, the crude compositions of my earliest boyhood. They
are printed *verbatim* – without alteration from the original
edition – the date of which is too remote to be judiciously
acknowledged.

E. A. P.

THE RAVEN

Once upon a midnight dreary, while I pondered, weak
    and weary,
Over many a quaint and curious volume of forgotten lore –
While I nodded, nearly napping, suddenly there came a
    tapping,
As of some one gently rapping, rapping at my chamber
    door.
"'Tis some visiter," I muttered, "tapping at my
    chamber door –
        Only this and nothing more."

Ah, distinctly I remember it was in the bleak December;
And each separate dying ember wrought its ghost
    upon the floor.
Eagerly I wished the morrow; – vainly I had sought
    to borrow
From my books surcease of sorrow – sorrow for the
    lost Lenore –
For the rare and radiant maiden whom the angels
    name Lenore –
        Nameless *here* for evermore.

And the silken, sad, uncertain rustling of each purple
    curtain
Thrilled me – filled me with fantastic terrors never felt
    before;
So that now, to still the beating of my heart, I stood
    repeating
" 'Tis some visiter entreating entrance at my chamber
    door –
Some late visiter entreating entrance at my chamber door; –
    This it is and nothing more."

Presently my soul grew stronger; hesitating then no
    longer,
"Sir," said I, "or Madam, truly your forgiveness I implore;
But the fact is I was napping, and so gently you came
    rapping,
And so faintly you came tapping, tapping at my
    chamber door,
That I scarce was sure I heard you" – here I opened
    wide the door; –
    Darkness there and nothing more.

Deep into that darkness peering, long I stood there
     wondering, fearing,
Doubting, dreaming dreams no mortal ever dared to
     dream before;
But the silence was unbroken, and the stillness gave no
     token,
And the only word there spoken was the whispered
     word, "Lenore?"
This I whispered, and an echo murmured back the
     word, "Lenore!"
       Merely this and nothing more.

Back into the chamber turning, all my soul within me
     burning,
Soon again I heard a tapping somewhat louder than before.
"Surely," said I, "surely that is something at my
     window lattice;
Let me see, then, what thereat is, and this mystery
     explore —
Let my heart be still a moment and this mystery explore; —
     'Tis the wind and nothing more!"

Open here I flung the shutter, when, with many a flirt
and flutter,
In there stepped a stately Raven of the saintly days of
yore;
Not the least obeisance made he; not a minute stopped
or stayed he;
But, with mien of lord or lady, perched above my
chamber door –
Perched upon a bust of Pallas just above my chamber
door –
Perched, and sat, and nothing more.

Then this ebony bird beguiling my sad fancy into smiling,
By the grave and stern decorum of the countenance it
wore,
"Though thy crest be shorn and shaven, thou," I said,
"art sure no craven,
Ghastly grim and ancient Raven wandering from the
Nightly shore –
Tell me what thy lordly name is on the Night's
Plutonian shore!"
Quoth the Raven "Nevermore."

Much I marvelled this ungainly fowl to hear discourse
    so plainly,
Though its answer little meaning – little relevancy bore;
For we cannot help agreeing that no living human being
Ever yet was blessed with seeing bird above his
    chamber door –
Bird or beast upon the sculptured bust above his
    chamber door,
        With such name as "Nevermore."

But the Raven, sitting lonely on the placid bust, spoke
    only
That one word, as if his soul in that one word he did
    outpour.
Nothing farther then he uttered – not a feather then he
    fluttered –
Till I scarcely more than muttered "Other friends have
    flown before –
On the morrow *he* will leave me, as my Hopes have
    flown before."
        Then the bird said "Nevermore."

Startled at the stillness broken by reply so aptly spoken,
"Doubtless," said I, "what it utters is its only stock and
    store
Caught from some unhappy master whom unmerciful
    Disaster
Followed fast and followed faster till his songs one
    burden bore —
Till the dirges of his Hope that melancholy burden
    bore
        Of 'Never — nevermore.' "

But the Raven still beguiling my sad fancy into
    smiling,
Straight I wheeled a cushioned seat in front of bird,
    and bust and door;
Then, upon the velvet sinking, I betook myself to
    linking
Fancy unto fancy, thinking what this ominous bird of
    yore —
What this grim, ungainly, ghastly, gaunt, and ominous
    bird of yore
        Meant in croaking "Nevermore."

This I sat engaged in guessing, but no syllable
    expressing
To the fowl whose fiery eyes now burned into my
    bosom's core;
This and more I sat divining, with my head at ease
    reclining
On the cushion's velvet lining that the lamp-light
    gloated o'er,
But whose velvet-violet lining with the lamp-light
    gloating o'er,
       She shall press, ah, nevermore!

Then, methought, the air grew denser, perfumed from
    an unseen censer
Swung by seraphim whose foot-falls tinkled on the
    tufted floor.
"Wretch," I cried, "thy God hath lent thee – by these
    angels he hath sent thee
Respite – respite and nepenthe from thy memories of
    Lenore;
Quaff, oh quaff this kind nepenthe and forget this lost
    Lenore!"
       Quoth the Raven "Nevermore."

"Prophet!" said I, "thing of evil! – prophet still, if bird
    or devil! –
Whether Tempter sent, or whether tempest tossed
    thee here ashore,
Desolate yet all undaunted, on this desert land
    enchanted –
On this home by Horror haunted – tell me truly,
    I implore –
Is there – *is* there balm in Gilead? – tell me – tell me,
    I implore!"
        Quoth the Raven "Nevermore."

"Prophet!" said I, "thing of evil! – prophet still, if bird
    or devil!
By that Heaven that bends above us – by that God we
    both adore –
Tell this soul with sorrow laden if, within the distant
    Aidenn,
It shall clasp a sainted maiden whom the angels name
    Lenore –
Clasp a rare and radiant maiden whom the angels name
    Lenore."
        Quoth the Raven "Nevermore."

"Be that word our sign of parting, bird or fiend!" I
    shrieked, upstarting –
"Get thee back into the tempest and the Night's
    Plutonian shore!
Leave no black plume as a token of that lie thy soul
    hath spoken!
Leave my loneliness unbroken! – quit the bust above
    my door!
Take thy beak from out my heart, and take thy form
    from off my door!"
        Quoth the Raven "Nevermore."

And the Raven, never flitting, still is sitting, *still* is
    sitting
On the pallid bust of Pallas just above my chamber
    door;
And his eyes have all the seeming of a demon's that is
    dreaming,
And the lamp–light o'er him streaming throws his
    shadow on the floor;
And my soul from out that shadow that lies floating on
    the floor
        Shall be lifted – nevermore!

AN ENIGMA

"Seldom we find," says Solomon Don Dunce,
    "Half an idea in the profoundest sonnet.
Through all the flimsy things we see at once
    As easily as through a Naples bonnet —
    Trash of all trash! — how *can* a lady don it?
Yet heavier far than your Petrarchan stuff —
Owl-downy nonsense that the faintest puff
    Twirls into trunk-paper the while you con it."
And, veritably, Sol is right enough.
The general tuckermanities are arrant
Bubbles — ephemeral and *so* transparent —
    But *this* is, now, — you may depend upon it —
Stable, opaque, immortal — all by dint
Of the dear names that lie concealed within 't.

ULALUME – A BALLAD

The skies they were ashen and sober;
    The leaves they were crispéd and sere –
    The leaves they were withering and sere:
It was night, in the lonesome October
    Of my most immemorial year:
It was hard by the dim lake of Auber,
    In the misty mid region of Weir: –
It was down by the dank tarn of Auber,
    In the ghoul-haunted woodland of Weir.

Here once, through an alley Titanic,
    Of cypress, I roamed with my Soul –
    Of cypress, with Psyche, my Soul.
These were days when my heart was volcanic
    As the scoriac rivers that roll –
    As the lavas that restlessly roll
Their sulphurous currents down Yaanek,
    In the ultimate climes of the Pole –
That groan as they roll down Mount Yaanek,
    In the realms of the Boreal Pole.

Our talk had been serious and sober,
    But our thoughts they were palsied and sere –
    Our memories were treacherous and sere;
For we knew not the month was October,

And we marked not the night of the year –
   (Ah, night of all nights in the year!)
We noted not the dim lake of Auber,
   (Though once we had journeyed down here)
We remembered not the dank tarn of Auber,
   Nor the ghoul-haunted woodland of Weir.

And now, as the night was senescent,
   And star-dials pointed to morn –
   As the star-dials hinted of morn –
At the end of our path a liquescent
   And nebulous lustre was born,
Out of which a miraculous crescent
   Arose with a duplicate horn –
Astarte's bediamonded crescent,
   Distinct with its duplicate horn.

And I said – "She is warmer than Dian;
   She rolls through an ether of sighs –
   She revels in a region of sighs.
She has seen that the tears are not dry on
   These cheeks where the worm never dies,
And has come past the stars of the Lion,
   To point us the path to the skies –
   To the Lethean peace of the skies –
Come up, in despite of the Lion,
   To shine on us with her bright eyes –

Come up, through the lair of the Lion,
    With love in her luminous eyes."

But Psyche, uplifting her finger,
    Said – "Sadly this star I mistrust –
    Her pallor I strangely mistrust –
Ah, hasten! – ah, let us not linger!
    Ah, fly! – let us fly! – for we must."
In terror she spoke; letting sink her
    Wings till they trailed in the dust –
In agony sobbed; letting sink her
    Plumes till they trailed in the dust –
    Till they sorrowfully trailed in the dust.

I replied – "This is nothing but dreaming.
    Let us on, by this tremulous light!
    Let us bathe in this crystalline light!
Its Sibyllic splendor is beaming
    With Hope and in Beauty to-night –
    See! – it flickers up the sky through the night!
Ah, we safely may trust to its gleaming
    And be sure it will lead us aright –
We surely may trust to a gleaming
    That cannot but guide us aright
Since it flickers up to Heaven through the night."

Thus I pacified Psyche and kissed her,
    And tempted her out of her gloom –
    And conquered her scruples and gloom;
And we passed to the end of the vista –
    But were stopped by the door of a tomb –
    By the door of a legended tomb: –
And I said – "What is written, sweet sister,
    On the door of this legended tomb?"
    She replied – "Ulalume – Ulalume! –
    'T is the vault of thy lost Ulalume!"

Then my heart it grew ashen and sober
    As the leaves that were crispéd and sere –
    As the leaves that were withering and sere –
And I cried – "It was surely October,
    On *this* very night of last year,
    That I journeyed – I journeyed down here! –
    That I brought a dread burden down here –
    On this night, of all nights in the year,
    Ah, what demon hath tempted me here?
Well I know, now, this dim lake of Auber –
    This misty mid region of Weir: –
Well I know, now, this dank tarn of Auber –
    This ghoul-haunted woodland of Weir."

Said we, then – the two, then – "Ah, can it
    Have been that the woodlandish ghouls –

The pitiful, the merciful ghouls,
To bar up our way and to ban it
From the secret that lies in these wolds –
From the thing that lies hidden in these wolds –
Have drawn up the spectre of a planet
From the limbo of lunary souls –
This sinfully scintillant planet
From the Hell of the planetary souls?"

TO MY MOTHER

Because I feel that, in the Heavens above,
  The angels, whispering to one another,
Can find, among their burning terms of love,
  None so devotional as that of "Mother,"
Therefore by that dear name I long have called you –
  You who are more than mother unto me,
And fill my heart of hearts, where Death installed you
  In setting my Virginia's spirit free.
My mother – my own mother, who died early,
  Was but the mother of myself; but you
Are mother to the one I loved so dearly,
  And thus are dearer than the mother I knew
By that infinity with which my wife
  Was dearer to my soul than its soul-life.

ELDORADO

Gaily bedight,
A gallant knight,
In sunshine and in shadow,
Had journeyed long,
Singing a song,
In search of Eldorado.

But he grew old –
This knight so bold –
And o'er his heart a shadow
Fell, as he found
No spot of ground
That looked like Eldorado.

    And, as his strength
    Failed him at length,
He met a pilgrim shadow –
    "Shadow," said he,
    "Where can it be –
This land of Eldorado?"

    "Over the Mountains
    Of the Moon,
Down the Valley of the Shadow,
    Ride, boldly ride,"
    The shade replied, –
"If you seek for Eldorado!"

THE VALLEY OF UNREST

Once it smiled a silent dell
Where the people did not dwell;
They had gone unto the wars,
Trusting to the mild-eyed stars,
Nightly, from their azure towers,
To keep watch above the flowers,
In the midst of which all day
The red sun-light lazily lay.
Now each visitor shall confess
The sad valley's restlessness.
Nothing there is motionless –
Nothing save the airs that brood
Over the magic solitude.
Ah, by no wind are stirred those trees
That palpitate like the chill seas
Around the misty Hebrides!

Ah, by no wind those clouds are driven
That rustle through the unquiet Heaven
Uneasily, from morn till even,
Over the violets there that lie
In myriad types of the human eye —
Over the lilies there that wave
And weep above a nameless grave!
They wave: — from out their fragrant tops
Eternal dews come down in drops.
They weep: — from off their delicate stems
Perennial tears descend in gems.

THE HAUNTED PALACE

In the greenest of our valleys
   By good angels tenanted,
Once a fair and stately palace –
   Radiant palace – reared its head.
In the monarch Thought's dominion –
   It stood there!
Never seraph spread a pinion
   Over fabric half so fair!

Banners yellow, glorious, golden,
   On its roof did float and flow –
(This – all this – was in the olden
   Time long ago)
And every gentle air that dallied,
   In that sweet day,
Along the ramparts plumed and pallid,
   A wingéd odor went away.

Wanderers in that happy valley,
    Through two luminous windows, saw
Spirits moving musically,
    To a lute's well-tunéd law,
Round about a throne where, sitting,
    Porphyrogene,
In state his glory well befitting
    The ruler of the realm was seen.

And all with pearl and ruby glowing
    Was the fair palace door,
Through which came flowing, flowing, flowing,
    And sparkling evermore,
A troop of Echoes whose sweet duty
    Was but to sing,
In voices of surpassing beauty,
    The wit and wisdom of their king.

But evil things, in robes of sorrow,
    Assailed the monarch's high estate.
(Ah, let us mourn! – for never morrow
    Shall dawn upon him, desolate!)
And round about his home the glory
    That blushed and bloomed,
Is but a dim-remembered story
    Of the old-time entombed.

And travellers, now, within that valley,
    Through the encrimsoned windows see
Vast forms that move fantastically
    To a discordant melody,
While, like a ghastly rapid river,
    Through the pale door
A hideous throng rush out forever
    And laugh – but smile no more.

THE CITY IN THE SEA

Lo! Death has reared himself a throne
In a strange city lying alone
Far down within the dim West,
Where the good and the bad and the worst and the best
Have gone to their eternal rest.
There shrines and palaces and towers
(Time-eaten towers that tremble not!)
Resemble nothing that is ours.
Around, by lifting winds forgot,
Resignedly beneath the sky
The melancholy waters lie.

No rays from the holy heaven come down
On the long night-time of that town;
But light from out the lurid sea
Streams up the turrets silently –
Gleams up the pinnacles far and free –
Up domes – up spires – up kingly halls –
Up fanes – up Babylon-like walls –
Up shadowy long-forgotten bowers
Of sculptured ivy and stone flowers –
Up many and many a marvellous shrine
Whose wreathéd friezes intertwine
The viol, the violet, and the vine.

Resignedly beneath the sky
The melancholy waters lie.
So blend the turrets and shadows there
That all seem pendulous in air,
While from a proud tower in the town
Death looks gigantically down.

There open fanes and gaping graves
Yawn level with the luminous waves;
But not the riches there that lie
In each idol's diamond eye –
Not the gaily-jewelled dead
Tempt the waters from their bed;
For no ripples curl, alas!
Along that wilderness of glass –
No swellings tell that winds may be
Upon some far-off happier sea –
No heavings hint that winds have been
On seas less hideously serene.

But lo, a stir is in the air!
The wave – there is a movement there!
As if the towers had thrust aside,
In slightly sinking, the dull tide –
As if their tops had feebly given
A void within the filmy Heaven.
The waves have now a redder glow –

The hours are breathing faint and low —
And when, amid no earthly moans,
Down, down that town shall settle hence.
Hell, rising from a thousand thrones,
Shall do it reverence.

THE BELLS

1

Hear the sledges with the bells –
  Silver bells!
What a world of merriment their melody foretells!
  How they tinkle, tinkle, tinkle,
    In the icy air of night!
  While the stars that oversprinkle
  All the Heavens, seem to twinkle
    With a crystalline delight;
  Keeping time, time, time,
  In a sort of Runic rhyme,
To the tintinabulation that so musically wells
  From the bells, bells, bells, bells,
    Bells, bells, bells –
  From the jingling and the tinkling of the bells.

2

Hear the mellow wedding bells –
  Golden bells!
What a world of happiness their harmony foretells!
  Through the balmy air of night
  How they ring out their delight! –
    From the molten-golden notes
    And all in tune,
  What a liquid ditty floats

To the turtle-dove that listens while she gloats
     On the moon!
   Oh, from out the sounding cells
What a gush of euphony voluminously wells!
     How it swells!
     How it dwells
   On the Future! – how it tells
   Of the rapture that impels
To the swinging and the ringing
   Of the bells, bells, bells! –
Of the bells, bells, bells, bells,
   Bells, bells, bells –
To the rhyming and the chiming of the bells!

       3
   Hear the loud alarum bells –
     Brazen bells!
What tale of terror, now, their turbulency tells!
   In the startled ear of Night
  How they scream out their affright!
   Too much horrified to speak,
   They can only shriek, shriek,
     Out of tune,
In a clamorous appealing to the mercy of the fire –
In a mad expostulation with the deaf and frantic fire,
   Leaping higher, higher, higher,
   With a desperate desire

And a resolute endeavor
Now – now to sit, or never,
By the side of the pale-faced moon.
Oh, the bells, bells, bells!
What a tale their terror tells
Of despair!
How they clang and clash and roar!
What a horror they outpour
In the bosom of the palpitating air!
Yet the ear, it fully knows,
By the twanging
And the clanging,
How the danger ebbs and flows: –
Yes, the ear distinctly tells,
In the jangling
And the wrangling,
How the danger sinks and swells,
By the sinking or the swelling in the anger of the bells –
Of the bells –
Of the bells, bells, bells, bells,
Bells, bells, bells –
In the clamor and the clangor of the bells.

Hear the tolling of the bells –
Iron bells!
What a world of solemn thought their monody compels!
In the silence of the night
How we shiver with affright
At the melancholy meaning of the tone!
For every sound that floats
From the rust within their throats
Is a groan.
And the people – ah, the people
They that dwell up in the steeple
All alone,
And who, tolling, tolling, tolling,
In that muffled monotone,
Feel a glory in so rolling
On the human heart a stone –
They are neither man nor woman –
They are neither brute nor human,
They are Ghouls: –
And their king it is who tolls: –
And he rolls, rolls, rolls, rolls
A Pæan from the bells!
And his merry bosom swells
With the Pæan of the bells!
And he dances and he yells;
Keeping time, time, time,

In a sort of Runic rhyme,
  To the Pæan of the bells —
    Of the bells: —
Keeping time, time, time,
In a sort of Runic rhyme,
  To the throbbing of the bells: —
Of the bells, bells, bells —
    To the sobbing of the bells:—
Keeping time, time, time,
    As he knells, knells, knells,
In a happy Runic rhyme,
  To the rolling of the bells —
Of the bells, bells, bells: —
  To the tolling of the bells —
Of the bells, bells, bells, bells,
    Bells, bells, bells —
To the moaning and the groaning of the bells.

AL AARAAF[1]

PART I

O! nothing earthly save the ray
(Thrown back from flowers) of Beauty's eye,
As in those gardens where the day
Springs from the gems of Circassy –
O! nothing earthly save the thrill
Of melody in woodland rill –
Or (music of the passion-hearted)
Joy's voice so peacefully departed
That like the murmur in the shell,
Its echo dwelleth and will dwell –
Oh, nothing of the dross of ours –
Yet all the beauty – all the flowers
That list our Love, and deck our bowers –
Adorn yon world afar, afar –
The wandering star.

'Twas a sweet time for Nesace – for there
Her world lay lolling on the golden air,
Near four bright suns – a temporary rest –
An oasis in desert of the blest.
Away – away – 'mid seas of rays that roll
Empyrean splendor o'er th' unchained soul –
The soul that scarce (the billows are so dense)
Can struggle to its destin'd eminence –

To distant spheres, from time to time, she rode,
And late to ours, the favour'd one of God –
But, now, the ruler of an anchor'd realm,
She throws aside the sceptre – leaves the helm,
And, amid incense and high spiritual hymns,
Laves in quadruple light her angel limbs.

    Now happiest, loveliest in yon lovely Earth,
Whence sprang the "Idea of Beauty" into birth,
(Falling in wreaths thro' many a startled star,
Like woman's hair 'mid pearls, until, afar,
It lit on hills Achaian, and there dwelt)
She look'd into Infinity – and knelt.
Rich clouds, for canopies, about her curled –
Fit emblems of the model of her world –
Seen but in beauty – not impeding sight
Of other beauty glittering thro' the light –
A wreath that twined each starry form around,
And all the opal'd air in color bound.

    All hurriedly she knelt upon a bed
Of flowers: of lilies such as rear'd the head
On the fair Capo Deucato, and sprang[2]
So eagerly around about to hang
Upon the flying footsteps of – deep pride –
Of her who lov'd a mortal – and so died.[3]
The Sephalica, budding with young bees,

128

Uprear'd its purple stem around her knees:
And gemmy flower,[4] of Trebizond misnam'd –
Inmate of highest stars, where erst it sham'd
All other loveliness: its honied dew
(The fabled nectar that the heathen knew)
Deliriously sweet, was dropp'd from Heaven,
And fell on gardens of the unforgiven
In Trebizond – and on a sunny flower
So like its own above that, to this hour,
It still remaineth, torturing the bee
With madness, and unwonted reverie:
In Heaven, and all its environs, the leaf
And blossom of the fairy plant, in grief
Disconsolate linger – grief that hangs her head,
Repenting follies that full long have fled,
Heaving her white breast to the balmy air,
Like guilty beauty, chasten'd, and more fair:
Nyctanthes too, as sacred as the light
She fears to perfume, perfuming the night:
And Clytia[5] pondering between many a sun,
While pettish tears adown her petals run:
And that aspiring flower[6] that sprang on Earth –
And died, ere scarce exalted into birth,
Bursting its odorous heart in spirit to wing
Its way to Heaven, from garden of a king:
And Valisnerian[7] lotus thither flown
From struggling with the waters of the Rhone:

And thy most lovely purple perfume,[8] Zante!
Isola d'oro! – Fior di Levante!
And the Nelumbo bud that floats for ever[9]
With Indian Cupid down the holy river –
Fair flowers, and fairy! to whose care is given
To bear the Goddess' song, in odors,[10] up to Heaven:

"Spirit! that dwellest where,
    In the deep sky,
The terrible and fair,
    In beauty vie!
Beyond the line of blue –
    The boundary of the star
Which turneth at the view
    Of thy barrier and thy bar –
Of the barrier overgone
    By the comets who were cast
From their pride, and from their throne
    To be drudges till the last –
To be carriers of fire
    (The red fire of their heart)
With speed that may not tire
    And with pain that shall not part –
Who livest – *that* we know –
    In Eternity – we feel –
But the shadow of whose brow
    What spirit shall reveal?

Tho' the beings whom thy Nesace,
   Thy messenger hath known
Have dream'd for thy Infinity
   A model of their own – [11]
Thy will is done, Oh, God!
   The star hath ridden high
Thro' many a tempest, but she rode
   Beneath thy burning eye;
And here, in thought, to thee –
   In thought that can alone
Ascend thy empire and so be
   A partner of thy throne –
By winged Fantasy,[12]
   My embassy is given,
Till secrecy shall knowledge be
   In the environs of Heaven."

She ceas'd – and buried then her burning cheek
Abash'd, amid the lilies there, to seek
A shelter from the fervour of His eye;
For the stars trembled at the Deity.
She stirr'd not – breath'd not – for a voice was there
How solemnly pervading the calm air!
A sound of silence on the startled ear
Which dreamy poets name "the music of the sphere."
Ours is a world of words: Quiet we call
"Silence" – which is the merest word of all.

131

All Nature speaks, and ev'n ideal things
Flap shadowy sounds from visionary wings –
But ah! not so when, thus, in realms on high
The eternal voice of God is passing by,
And the red winds are withering in the sky!

    "What tho' in worlds which sightless cycles run,[13]
Link'd to a little system, and one sun –
Where all my love is folly and the crowd
Still think my terrors but the thunder cloud,
The storm, the earthquake, and the ocean-wrath –
(Ah! will they cross me in my angrier path?)
What tho' in worlds which own a single sun
The sands of Time grow dimmer as they run,
Yet thine is my resplendency, so given
To bear my secrets thro' the upper Heaven.
Leave tenantless thy crystal home, and fly,
With all thy train, athwart the moony sky –
Apart – like fire-flies in Sicilian night,[14]
And wing to other worlds another light!
Divulge the secrets of thy embassy
To the proud orbs that twinkle – and so be
To ev'ry heart a barrier and a ban
Lest the stars totter in the guilt of man!"

    Up rose the maiden in the yellow night,
The single-mooned eve! – on Earth we plight

Our faith to one love – and one moon adore –
The birth-place of young Beauty had no more.
As sprang that yellow star from downy hours
Up rose the maiden from her shrine of flowers,
And bent o'er sheeny mountain and dim plain
Her way – but left not yet her Therasæan reign.[15]

PART II

High on a mountain of enamell'd head –
Such as the drowsy shepherd on his bed
Of giant pasturage lying at his ease,
Raising his heavy eyelid, starts and sees
With many a mutter'd "hope to be forgiven"
What time the moon is quadrated in Heaven –
Of rosy head, that towering far away
Into the sunlit ether, caught the ray
Of sunken suns at eve – at noon of night,
While the moon danc'd with the fair stranger light –
Uprear'd upon such height arose a pile
Of gorgeous columns on th' unburthen'd air,
Flashing from Parian marble that twin smile
Far down upon the wave that sparkled there,
And nursled the young mountain in its lair.
Of molten stars their pavement, such as fall[16]
Thro' the ebon air, besilvering the pall
Of their own dissolution, while they die –
Adorning then the dwellings of the sky.

A dome, by linked light from Heaven let down,
Sat gently on these columns as a crown –
A window of one circular diamond, there,
Look'd out above into the purple air,
And rays from God shot down that meteor chain
And hallow'd all the beauty twice again,
Save when, between th' Empyrean and that ring,
Some eager spirit flapp'd his dusky wing.
But on the pillars Seraph eyes have seen
The dimness of this world: that greyish green
That Nature loves the best for Beauty's grave
Lurk'd in each cornice, round each architrave –
And every sculptur'd cherub thereabout
That from his marble dwelling peeréd out,
Seem'd earthly in the shadow of his niche –
Achaian statues in a world so rich?
Friezes from Tadmor and Persepolis – [17]
From Balbec, and the stilly, clear abyss
Of beautiful Gomorrah! O, the wave[18]
Is now upon thee – but too late to save!

    Sound loves to revel in a summer night:
Witness the murmur of the grey twilight
That stole upon the ear, in Eyraco,[19]
Of many a wild star-gazer long ago –
That stealeth ever on the ear of him
Who, musing, gazeth on the distance dim,

And sees the darkness coming as a cloud –
Is not its form – its voice – most palpable and loud?[20]

    But what is this? – it cometh – and it brings
A music with it – 'tis the rush of wings –
A pause – and then a sweeping, falling strain
And Nesace is in her halls again.
From the wild energy of wanton haste
    Her cheeks were flushing, and her lips apart;
And zone that clung around her gentle waist
    Had burst beneath the heaving of her heart.
Within the centre of that hall to breathe
She paus'd and panted, Zanthe! all beneath,
The fairy light that kiss'd her golden hair
And long'd to rest, yet could but sparkle there!

    Young flowers were whispering in melody[21]
To happy flowers that night – and tree to tree;
Fountains were gushing music as they fell
In many a star-lit grove, or moon-lit dell;
Yet silence came upon material things –
Fair flowers, bright waterfalls and angel wings –
And sound alone that from the spirit sprang
Bore burthen to the charm the maiden sang:

        "'Neath blue-bell or streamer –
            Or tufted wild spray

That keeps, from the dreamer,
  The moonbeam away — [22]
Bright beings! that ponder,
  With half closing eyes,
On the stars which your wonder
  Hath drawn from the skies,
Till they glance thro' the shade, and
  Come down to your brow
Like — eyes of the maiden
  Who calls on you now —
Arise! from your dreaming
  In violet bowers,
To duty beseeming
  These star-litten hours —
And shake from your tresses
  Encumber'd with dew
The breath of those kisses
  That cumber them too —
(O! how, without you, Love!
  Could angels be blest?)
Those kisses of true love
  That lull'd ye to rest!
Up! — shake from your wing
  Each hindering thing:
The dew of the night —
  It would weigh down your flight;
And true love caresses —

O! leave them apart!
They are light on the tresses,
   But lead on the heart.

Ligeia! Ligeia!
   My beautiful one!
Whose harshest idea
   Will to melody run,
O! is it thy will
   On the breezes to toss?
Or, capriciously still,
   Like the lone Albatross,[23]
Incumbent on night
   (As she on the air)
To keep watch with delight
   On the harmony there?

Ligeia! wherever
   Thy image may be,
No magic shall sever
   Thy music from thee.
Thou hast bound many eyes
   In a dreamy sleep –
But the strains still arise
   Which *thy* vigilance keep –
The sound of the rain
   Which leaps down to the flower,

And dances again
  In the rhythm of the shower –
The murmur that springs[24]
  From the growing of grass
Are the music of things –
  But are modell'd, alas! –
Away, then my dearest,
  O! hie thee away
To springs that lie clearest
  Beneath the moon-ray –
To lone lake that smiles,
  In its dream of deep rest,
At the many star-isles
  That enjewel its breast –
Where wild flowers, creeping,
  Have mingled their shade,
On its margin is sleeping
  Full many a maid –
Some have left the cool glade, and
  Have slept with the bee –[25]
Arouse them my maiden,
  On moorland and lea –
Go! breathe on their slumber,
  All softly in ear,
The musical number
  They slumber'd to hear –
For what can awaken

>   An angel so soon
>   Whose sleep hath been taken
>   Beneath the cold moon,
>   As the spell which no slumber
>   Of witchery may test,
>   The rhythmical number
>   Which lull'd him to rest?"

Spirits in wing, and angels to the view,
A thousand seraphs burst th' Empyrean thro',
Young dreams still hovering on their drowsy flight –
Seraphs in all but "Knowledge," the keen light
That fell, refracted, thro' thy bounds, afar
O Death! from eye of God upon that star:
Sweet was that error – sweeter still that death –
Sweet was that error – ev'n with *us* the breath
Of Science dims the mirror of our joy –
To them 'twere the Simoom, and would destroy –
For what (to them) availeth it to know
That Truth is Falsehood – or that Bliss is Woe?
Sweet was their death – with them to die was rife
With the last ecstasy of satiate life –
Beyond that death no immortality –
But sleep that pondereth and is not "to be" –
And there – oh! may my weary spirit dwell –
Apart from Heaven's Eternity – and yet how far from
        Hell!²⁶

What guilty spirit, in what shrubbery dim,
Heard not the stirring summons of that hymn?
But two: they fell: for Heaven no grace imparts
To those who hear not for their beating hearts.
A maiden-angel and her seraph-lover –
O! where (and ye may seek the wide skies over)
Was Love, the blind, near sober Duty known?
Unguided Love hath fallen – 'mid "tears of perfect
     moan." [27]

  He was a goodly spirit – he who fell:
A wanderer by moss-y-mantled well –
A gazer on the lights that shine above –
A dreamer in the moonbeam by his love:
What wonder? for each star is eye-like there,
And looks so sweetly down on Beauty's hair –
And they, and ev'ry mossy spring were holy
To his love-haunted heart and melancholy.
The night had found (to him a night of wo)
Upon a mountain crag, young Angelo –
Beetling it bends athwart the solemn sky,
And scowls on starry worlds that down beneath it lie.
Here sate he with his love – his dark eye bent
With eagle gaze along the firmament:
Now turn'd it upon her – but ever then
It trembled to the orb of EARTH again.

"Ianthe, dearest, see! how dim that ray!
How lovely 'tis to look so far away!
She seem'd not thus upon that autumn eve
I left her gorgeous halls – nor mourn'd to leave.
That eve – that eve – I should remember well –
The sun-ray dropp'd, in Lemnos, with a spell
On th' Arabesque carving of a gilded hall
Wherein I sate, and on the draperied wall –
And on my eye-lids – O the heavy light!
How drowsily it weigh'd them into night!
On flowers, before, and mist, and love they ran
With Persian Saadi in his Gulistan:
But O that light! – I slumber'd – Death, the while,
Stole o'er my senses in that lovely isle
So softly that no single silken hair
Awoke that slept – or knew that he was there.
The last spot of Earth's orb I trod upon
Was a proud temple call'd the Parthenon – [28]
More beauty clung around her column'd wall
Than ev'n thy glowing bosom beats withal,[29]
And when old Time my wing did disenthral
Thence sprang I – as the eagle from his tower,
And years I left behind me in an hour.
What time upon her airy bounds I hung
One half the garden of her globe was flung
Unrolling as a chart unto my view –
Tenantless cities of the desert too!

Ianthe, beauty crowded on me then,
And half I wish'd to be again of men."

"My Angelo! and why of them to be?
A brighter dwelling-place is here for thee –
And greener fields than in yon world above,
And woman's loveliness – and passionate love."

"But, list, Ianthe! when the air so soft
Fail'd, as my pennon'd spirit leapt aloft,³⁰
Perhaps my brain grew dizzy – but the world
I left so late was into chaos hurl'd –
Sprang from her station, on the winds apart,
And roll'd, a flame, the fiery Heaven athwart.
Methought, my sweet one, then I ceased to soar
And fell – not swiftly as I rose before,
But with a downward, tremulous motion thro'
Light, brazen rays, this golden star unto!
Nor long the measure of my falling hours,
For nearest of all stars was thine to ours –
Dread star! that came, amid a night of mirth,
A red Dædalion on the timid Earth."

"We came – and to thy Earth – but not to us
Be given our lady's bidding to discuss:
We came, my love; around, above, below,
Gay fire-fly of the night we come and go,

142

Nor ask a reason save the angel-nod
She grants to us, as granted by her God –
But, Angelo, than thine grey Time unfurl'd
Never his fairy wing o'er fairier world!
Dim was its little disk, and angel eyes
Alone could see the phantom in the skies,
When first Al Aaraaf knew her course to be
Headlong thitherward o'er the starry sea –
But when its glory swell'd upon the sky,
As glowing Beauty's bust beneath man's eye,
We paus'd before the heritage of men,
And thy star trembled – as doth Beauty then!"

Thus, in discourse, the lovers whiled away
The night that waned and waned and brought no day.
They fell: for Heaven to them no hope imparts
Who hear not for the beating of their hearts.

1 A star was discovered by Tycho Brahe which appeared
suddenly in the heavens – attained, in a few days, a brilliancy
surpassing that of Jupiter – then as suddenly disappeared, and
has never been seen since.
2 On Santa Maura – olim Deucadia.
3 Sappho.
4 This flower is much noticed by Lewenhoeck and
Tournefort. The bee, feeding upon its blossom, becomes
intoxicated.

5 Clytia – The Chrysanthemum Peruvianum, or, to employ a better-known term, the turnsol – which turns continually towards the sun, covers itself, like Peru, the country from which it comes, with dewy clouds which cool and refresh its flowers during the most violent heat of the day – *B. de St. Pierre.*

6 There is cultivated in the king's garden at Paris, a species of serpentine aloes without prickles, whose large and beautiful flower exhales a strong odour of the vanilla, during the time of its expansion, which is very short. It does not blow till towards the month of July – you then perceive it gradually open its petals – expand them – fade and die. – *St. Pierre.*

7 There is found, in the Rhone, a beautiful lily of the Valisnerian kind. Its stem will stretch to the length of three or four feet – thus preserving its head above water in the swellings of the river.

8 The Hyacinth.

9 It is a fiction of the Indians, that Cupid was first seen floating in one of these down the river Ganges – and that he still loves the cradle of his childhood.

10 And golden vials full of odors which are the prayers of the saints. – *Rev. St. John.*

11 The Humanitarians held that God was to be understood as having really a human form. – *Vide Clarke's Sermons,* vol. 1, page 26, fol. edit.

The drift of Milton's argument, leads him to employ language which would appear, at first sight, to verge upon their doctrine; but it will be seen immediately, that he guards himself against the charge of having adopted one of the most ignorant errors of the dark ages of the church. – *Dr. Sumner's Notes on Milton's Christian Doctrine.*

This opinion, in spite of many testimonies to the contrary,

144

could never have been very general. Andeus, a Syrian of Mesopotamia, was condemned for the opinion, as heretical. He lived in the beginning of the fourth century. His disciples were called Anthropmorphites. – *Vide Du Pin.*

Among Milton's minor poems are these lines: –

  Dicite sacrorum præsides nemorum Deæ, &c.

  Quis ille primus cujus ex imagine

  Natura solers finxit humanum genus?

  Eternus, incorruptus, æquævus polo,

  Unusque et universus exemplar Dei. – And afterwards,

  Non cui profundum Cæcitas lumen dedit

  Dircæus augur vidit hunc alto sinu, &c.

12 Seltsamen Tochter Jovis

  Seinem Schosskinde

  Der Phantasie. – *Göethe.*

13 Sightless – too small to be seen. – *Legge.*

14 I have often noticed a peculiar movement of the fire-flies; – they will collect in a body and fly off, from a common centre, into innumerable radii.

15 Therasæa, or Therasea, the island mentioned by Seneca, which, in a moment, arose from the sea to the eyes of astonished mariners.

16 Some star which, from the ruin'd roof

  Of shak'd Olympus, by mischance, did fall. – *Milton.*

17 Voltaire, in speaking of Persepolis, says, "Je connois bien l'admiration qu'inspirent ces ruines – mais un palais erigé au pied d'une chaine des rochers sterils – peut il être un chef d'œuvre des arts!"

18 "Oh! the wave" – Ula Deguisi is the Turkish appellation; but, on its own shores, it is called Bahar Loth, or Almotanah. There were undoubtedly more than two cities engulphed in the "dead sea." In the valley of Siddim were five

– Adrah, Zeboin, Zoar, Sodom and Gomorrah. Stephen of Byzantium mentions eight, and Strabo thirteen, (engulphed) – but the last is out of all reason.

It is said, [Tacitus, Strabo, Josephus, Daniel of St. Saba, Nau, Maundrell, Troilo, D'Arvieux] that after an excessive drought, the vestiges of columns, walls, &c. are seen above the surface. At *any* season, such remains may be discovered by looking down into the transparent lake, and at such distances as would argue the existence of many settlements in the space now usurped by the "Asphaltites."

19 Eyraco – Chaldea.

20 I have often thought I could distinctly hear the sound of the darkness as it stole over the horizon.

21 Fairies use flowers for their charactery. – *Merry Wives of Windsor.*

22 In Scripture is this passage – "The sun shall not harm thee by day, nor the moon by night." It is perhaps not generally known that the moon, in Egypt, has the effect of producing blindness to those who sleep with the face exposed to its rays, to which circumstance the passage evidently alludes.

23 The Albatross is said to sleep on the wing.

24 I met with this idea in an old English tale, which I am now unable to obtain and quote from memory: – "The verie essence and, as it were, springe-heade and origine of all musiche is the verie pleasaunte sounde which the trees of the forest do make when they growe."

25 The wild bee will not sleep in the shade if there be moonlight.

The rhyme in this verse, as in one about sixty lines before, has an appearance of affectation. It is, however, imitated from Sir W. Scott, or rather from Claud Halcro – in whose mouth I admired its effect:

> O! were there an island,
>   Tho' ever so wild
> Where woman might smile, and
>   No man be beguil'd, &c.

26 With the Arabians there is a medium between Heaven and Hell, where men suffer no punishment, but yet do not attain that tranquil and even happiness which they suppose to be characteristic of heavenly enjoyment.

> Un no rompido sueno –
> Un dia puro – allegre – libre
> Quiera –
> Libre de amor – de zelo –
> De odio – de esperanza – de rezelo. – *Luis Ponce de Leon.*

Sorrow is not excluded from "Al Aaraaf," but it is that sorrow which the living love to cherish for the dead, and which, in some minds, resembles the delirium of opium. The passionate excitement of Love and the buoyancy of spirit attendant upon intoxication are its less holy pleasures – the price of which, to those souls who make choice of "Al Aaraaf" as their residence after life, is final death and annihilation.

27 There be tears of perfect moan
    Wept for thee in Helicon. – *Milton.*

28 It was entire in 1687 – the most elevated spot in Athens.

29 Shadowing more beauty in their airy brows
    Than have the white breasts of the Queen of Love. – *Marlowe.*

30 Pennon – for pinion. – *Milton.*

TAMERLANE

Kind solace in a dying hour!
   Such, father, is not (now) my theme –
I will not madly deem that power
      Of Earth may shrive me of the sin
      Unearthly pride hath revell'd in –
   I have no time to dote or dream:
You call it hope – that fire of fire!
It is but agony of desire:
   If I *can* hope – Oh God! I can –
   Its fount is holier – more divine –
I would not call thee fool, old man,
   But such is not a gift of thine.

Know thou the secret of a spirit
   Bow'd from its wild pride into shame.
O yearning heart! I did inherit
   Thy withering portion with the fame,
The searing glory which hath shone
Amid the Jewels of my throne,
Halo of Hell! and with a pain
Not Hell shall make me fear again –
O craving heart, for the lost flowers
And sunshine of my summer hours!
The undying voice of that dead time,
With its interminable chime,

Rings, in the spirit of a spell,
Upon thy emptiness – a knell.

I have not always been as now:
The fever'd diadem on my brow
 I claim'd and won usurpingly —
Hath not the same fierce heirdom given
 Rome to the Cæsar – this to me?
 The heritage of a kingly mind,
And a proud spirit which hath striven
 Triumphantly with human kind.

On mountain soil I first drew life:
 The mists of the Taglay have shed
 Nightly their dews upon my head,
And, I believe, the winged strife
And tumult of the headlong air
Have nestled in my very hair.

So late from Heaven – that dew – it fell
 ('Mid dreams of an unholy night)
Upon me with the touch of Hell,
 While the red flashing of the light
From clouds that hung, like banners, o'er,
 Appeared to my half-closing eye

The pageantry of monarchy,
And the deep trumpet-thunder's roar
    Came hurriedly upon me, telling
        Of human battle, where my voice,
    My own voice, silly child! – was swelling
        (O! how my spirit would rejoice,
And leap within me at the cry)
The battle-cry of Victory!

The rain came down upon my head
    Unshelter'd – and the heavy wind
    Rendered me mad and deaf and blind.
It was but man, I thought, who shed
    Laurels upon me: and the rush –
The torrent of the chilly air
Gurgled within my ear the crush
    Of empires – with the captive's prayer –
The hum of suitors – and the tone
Of flattery 'round a sovereign's throne.

My passions, from that hapless hour,
    Usurp'd a tyranny which men
Have deem'd, since I have reach'd to power,
        My innate nature – be it so:
    But, father, there liv'd one who, then,
Then – in my boyhood – when their fire
        Burn'd with a still intenser glow

(For passion must, with youth, expire)
 E'en *then* who knew this iron heart
 In woman's weakness had a part.

I have no words – alas! – to tell
The loveliness of loving well!
Nor would I now attempt to trace
The more than beauty of a face
Whose lineaments, upon my mind,
Are — shadows on th' unstable wind:
Thus I remember having dwelt
 Some page of early lore upon,
With loitering eye, till I have felt
The letters – with their meaning – melt
 To fantasies – with none.

O, she was worthy of all love!
 Love – as in infancy was mine –
'Twas such as angel minds above
 Might envy; her young heart the shrine
On which my every hope and thought
 Were incense – then a goodly gift,
  For they were childish and upright –
Pure — as her young example taught:
 Why did I leave it, and, adrift,
  Trust to the fire within, for light?

We grew in age – and love – together –
   Roaming the forest, and the wild;
My breast her shield in wintry weather –
   And, when the friendly sunshine smil'd,
And she would mark the opening skies,
I saw no Heaven – but in her eyes.

Young Love's first lesson is — the heart:
   For 'mid that sunshine, and those smiles,
When, from our little cares apart,
   And laughing at her girlish wiles,
I'd throw me on her throbbing breast,
   And pour my spirit out in tears –
There was no need to speak the rest –
   No need to quiet any fears
Of her – who ask'd no reason why,
But turn'd on me her quiet eye!

Yet *more* than worthy of the love
My spirit struggled with, and strove,
When, on the mountain peak, alone,
Ambition lent it a new tone –
I had no being – but in thee:
   The world, and all it did contain
In the earth – the air – the sea –
   Its joy – its little lot of pain
That was new pleasure — the ideal,

Dim, vanities of dreams by night –
And dimmer nothings which were real –
   (Shadows – and a more shadowy light!)
Parted upon their misty wings,
      And, so, confusedly, became
      Thine image and – a name – a name!
Two separate – yet most intimate things.

I was ambitious – have you known
      The passion, father? You have not:
A cottager, I mark'd a throne
Of half the world as all my own,
      And murmur'd at such lowly lot –
But, just like any other dream,
      Upon the vapor of the dew
My own had past, did not the beam
      Of beauty which did while it thro'
The minute – the hour – the day – oppress
My mind with double loveliness.

We walk'd together on the crown
Of a high mountain which look'd down
Afar from its proud natural towers
   Of rock and forest, on the hills –
The dwindled hills! begirt with bowers
   And shouting with a thousand rills.

I spoke to her of power and pride,
    But mystically – in such guise
That she might deem it nought beside
    The moment's converse; in her eyes
I read, perhaps too carelessly –
    A mingled feeling with my own –
The flush on her bright cheek, to me
    Seem'd to become a queenly throne
Too well that I should let it be
    Light in the wilderness alone.

I wrapp'd myself in grandeur then
    And donn'd a visionary crown —
        Yet it was not that Fantasy
        Had thrown her mantle over me –
But that, among the rabble – men,
        Lion ambition is chain'd down –
And crouches to a keeper's hand –
Not so in deserts where the grand –
The wild – the terrible conspire
With their own breath to fan his fire.

Look 'round thee now on Samarcand! –
    Is she not queen of Earth? her pride
Above all cities? in her hand
    Their destinies? in all beside
Of glory which the world hath known

Stands she not nobly and alone?
Falling – her veriest stepping-stone
Shall form the pedestal of a throne –
And who her sovereign? Timour – he
    Whom the astonished people saw
Striding o'er empires haughtily
    A diadem'd outlaw!

O, human love! thou spirit given,
On Earth, of all we hope in Heaven!
Which fall'st into the soul like rain
Upon the Siroc-wither'd plain,
And, failing in thy power to bless,
But leav'st the heart a wilderness!
Idea! which bindest life around
With music of so strange a sound
And beauty of so wild a birth –
Farewell! for I have won the Earth.

When Hope, the eagle that tower'd, could see
    No cliff beyond him in the sky,
His pinions were bent droopingly –
    And homeward turn'd his soften'd eye.
'Twas sunset: when the sun will part
There comes a sullenness of heart
To him who still would look upon
The glory of the summer sun.

That soul will hate the ev'ning mist
So often lovely, and will list
To the sound of the coming darkness (known
To those whose spirits harken) as one
Who, in a dream of night, *would* fly
But *cannot* from a danger nigh.

What tho' the moon – the white moon
Shed all the splendor of her noon,
Her smile is chilly – and *her* beam,
In that time of dreariness, will seem
(So like you gather in your breath)
A portrait taken after death.
And boyhood is a summer sun
Whose waning is the dreariest one –
For all we live to know is known
And all we seek to keep hath flown –
Let life, then, as the day-flower, fall
With the noon-day beauty – which is all.

I reach'd my home – my home no more –
    For all had flown who made it so.
I pass'd from out its mossy door,
    And, tho' my tread was soft and low,
A voice came from the threshold stone
Of one whom I had earlier known –
    O, I defy thee, Hell, to show

On beds of fire that burn below,
   An humbler heart — a deeper wo.
Father, I firmly do believe —
   I *know* — for Death who comes for me
      From regions of the blest afar,
Where there is nothing to deceive,
      Hath left his iron gate ajar,
   And rays of truth you cannot see
   Are flashing thro' Eternity —
I do believe that Eblis hath
A snare in every human path —
Else how, when in the holy grove
I wandered of the idol, Love,
Who daily scents his snowy wings
With incense of burnt offerings
From the most unpolluted things,
Whose pleasant bowers are yet so riven
Above with trellic'd rays from Heaven
No mote may shun — no tiniest fly —
The light'ning of his eagle eye —
How was it that Ambition crept,
   Unseen, amid the revels there,
Till growing bold, he laughed and leapt
   In the tangles of Love's very hair?

SELECTED PROSE

THE PHILOSOPHY OF COMPOSITION

Charles Dickens, in a note now lying before me, alluding to an examination I once made of the mechanism of "Barnaby Rudge," says – "By the way, are you aware that Godwin wrote his 'Caleb Williams' backwards? He first involved his hero in a web of difficulties, forming the second volume, and then, for the first, cast about him for some mode of accounting for what had been done."

I cannot think this the *precise* mode of procedure on the part of Godwin – and indeed what he himself acknowledges, is not altogether in accordance with Mr. Dickens' idea – but the author of "Caleb Williams" was too good an artist not to perceive the advantage derivable from at least a somewhat similar process. Nothing is more clear than that every plot, worth the name, must be elaborated to its *dénouement* before any thing be attempted with the pen. It is only with the *dénouement* constantly in view that we can give a plot its indispensable air of consequence, or causation, by making the incidents, and especially the tone at all points, tend to the development of the intention.

There is a radical error, I think, in the usual mode of constructing a story. Either history affords a thesis – or one is suggested by an incident of the day – or, at best, the author sets himself to work in the combination of

161

striking events to form merely the basis of his narrative – designing, generally, to fill in with description, dialogue, or autorial comment, whatever crevices of fact, or action, may, from page to page, render themselves apparent.

I prefer commencing with the consideration of an *effect.* Keeping originality *always* in view – for he is false to himself who ventures to dispense with so obvious and so easily attainable a source of interest – I say to myself, in the first place, "Of the innumerable effects, or impressions, of which the heart, the intellect, or (more generally) the soul is susceptible, what one shall I, on the present occasion, select?" Having chosen a novel, first, and secondly a vivid effect, I consider whether it can best be wrought by incident or tone – whether by ordinary incidents and peculiar tone, or the converse, or by peculiarity both of incident and tone – afterward looking about me (or rather within) for such combinations of event, or tone, as shall best aid me in the construction of the effect.

I have often thought how interesting a magazine paper might be written by any author who would – that is to say, who could – detail, step by step, the processes by which any one of his compositions attained its ultimate point of completion. Why such a paper has never been given to the world, I am much at a loss to say – but, perhaps, the autorial vanity has had more to do with the omission than any one other cause. Most writers – poets in especial – prefer having it understood that they compose by a species of fine frenzy – an ecstatic intuition – and would positively shudder at letting the public take a peep behind the scenes, at the elaborate and vacillating crudities of thought – at the true purposes seized only at the last moment – at the innumerable glimpses of idea that arrived not at the maturity of full view – at the fully matured fancies discarded in despair as unmanageable – at the cautious selections and rejections – at the painful erasures and interpolations – in a word, at the wheels and pinions – the tackle for scene-shifting – the step-ladders and demon-traps – the cock's feathers, the red paint and the black patches, which, in ninety-nine cases out of the hundred, constitute the properties of the literary *histrio*.

I am aware, on the other hand, that the case is by no means common, in which an author is at all in condition to retrace the steps by which his conclusions have been attained. In general, suggestions, having arisen pell-mell, are pursued and forgotten in a similar manner.

For my own part, I have neither sympathy with the repugnance alluded to, nor, at any time, the least difficulty in recalling to mind the progressive steps of any of my compositions; and, since the interest of an analysis, or reconstruction, such as I have considered a *desideratum*, is quite independent of any real or fancied

163

interest in the thing analyzed, it will not be regarded as a breach of decorum on my part to show the *modus operandi* by which some one of my own works was put together. I select "The Raven," as the most generally known. It is my design to render it manifest that no one point in its composition is referrible either to accident or intuition – that the work proceeded, step by step, to its completion with the precision and rigid consequence of a mathematical problem.

Let us dismiss, as irrelevant to the poem *per se*, the circumstance – or say the necessity – which, in the first place, gave rise to the intention of composing a poem that should suit at once the popular and the critical taste.

We commence, then, with this intention.

The initial consideration was that of extent. If any literary work is too long to be read at one sitting, we must be content to dispense with the immensely important effect derivable from unity of impression – for, if two sittings be required, the affairs of the world interfere, and every thing like totality is at once destroyed. But since, *ceteris paribus*, no poet can afford to dispense with *any thing* that may advance his design, it but remains to be seen whether there is, in extent, any advantage to counterbalance the loss of unity which attends it. Here I say no, at once. What we term a long poem is, in fact, merely a succession of brief ones – that is to say, of brief poetical effects. It is needless to demonstrate that a poem is such, only inasmuch as it intensely excites, by elevating, the soul; and all intense excitements are, through a psychal necessity, brief. For this reason, at least one half of the "Paradise Lost" is essentially prose – a succession of poetical excitements interspersed, *inevitably*, with corresponding depressions – the whole being deprived, through the extremeness of its length, of the vastly important artistic element, totality, or unity, of effect.

It appears evident, then, that there is a distinct limit, as regards length, to all works of literary art – the limit of a single sitting – and that, although in certain classes of prose composition, such as "Robinson Crusoe," (demanding no unity,) this limit may be advantageously overpassed, it can never properly be overpassed in a poem. Within this limit, the extent of a poem may be made to bear mathematical relation to its merit – in other words, to the excitement or elevation – again in other words, to the degree of the true poetical effect which it is capable of inducing; for it is clear that the brevity must be in direct ratio of the intensity of the intended effect: – this, with one proviso – that a certain degree of duration is absolutely requisite for the production of any effect at all.

Holding in view these considerations, as well as that degree of excitement which I deemed not above the popular, while not below the critical, taste, I reached at once what I conceived the proper *length* for my intended poem – a length of about one hundred lines. It is, in fact, a hundred and eight.

My next thought concerned the choice of an impression, or effect, to be conveyed: and here I may as well observe that, throughout the construction, I kept steadily in view the design of rendering the work *universally* appreciable. I should be carried too far out of my immediate topic were I to demonstrate a point upon which I have repeatedly insisted, and which, with the poetical, stands not in the slightest need of demonstration – the point, I mean, that Beauty is the sole legitimate province of the poem. A few words, however, in elucidation of my real meaning, which some of my friends have evinced a disposition to misrepresent. That pleasure which is at once the most intense, the most elevating, and the most pure, is, I believe, found in the contemplation of the beautiful. When, indeed, men speak of Beauty, they mean, precisely, not a quality, as is supposed, but an effect – they refer, in short, just to that intense and pure elevation of *soul* – *not* of intellect, or of heart – upon which I have commented, and which is experienced in consequence of contemplating "the beautiful." Now I designate Beauty as the province of the poem, merely because it is an obvious rule of Art that effects should be made to spring from direct causes – that objects should be attained through means best adapted for their attainment – no one as yet having been weak enough to deny that the peculiar elevation alluded to, is *most readily* attained in the poem. Now the object, Truth, or the satisfaction of the intellect, and the object Passion, or the excitement of the heart, are, although attainable, to a certain extent, in poetry, far more readily attainable in prose. Truth, in fact, demands a precision, and Passion, a *homeliness* (the truly passionate will comprehend me) which are absolutely antagonistic to that Beauty which, I maintain, is the excitement, or pleasurable elevation, of the soul. It by no means follows from any thing here said, that passion, or even truth, may not be introduced, and even profitably introduced, into a poem – for they may serve in elucidation, or aid the general effect, as do discords in music, by contrast – but the true artist will always contrive, first, to tone them into proper subservience to the predominant aim, and, secondly, to enveil them, as far as possible, in that Beauty which is the atmosphere and the essence of the poem.

Regarding, then, Beauty as my province, my next question referred to the *tone* of its highest manifestation – and all experience has shown that this tone is one of *sadness*. Beauty of whatever kind, in its supreme development, invariably excites the sensitive soul to tears.

Melancholy is thus the most legitimate of all the poetical tones.

The length, the province, and the tone, being thus determined, I betook myself to ordinary induction, with the view of obtaining some artistic piquancy which might serve me as a key-note in the construction of the poem – some pivot upon which the whole structure might turn. In carefully thinking over all the usual artistic effects – or more properly *points*, in the theatrical sense – I did not fail to perceive immediately that no one had been so universally employed as that of the *refrain*. The universality of its employment sufficed to assure me of its intrinsic value, and spared me the necessity of submitting it to analysis. I considered it, however, with regard to its susceptibility of improvement, and soon saw it to be in a primitive condition. As commonly used, the *refrain*, or burden, not only is limited to lyric verse, but depends for its impression upon the force of monotone – both in sound and thought. The pleasure is deduced solely from the sense of identity – of repetition. I resolved to diversify, and so vastly heighten, the effect, by adhering, in general, to the monotone of sound, while I continually varied that of thought: that is to say, I determined to produce continuously novel effects, by the variation *of the application* of the *refrain* – the *refrain* itself remaining, for the most part, unvaried.

These points being settled, I next bethought me of the *nature* of my *refrain*. Since its application was to be repeatedly varied, it was clear that the *refrain* itself must be brief, for there would have been an insurmountable difficulty in frequent variations of application in any sentence of length. In proportion to the brevity of the sentence, would, of course, be the facility of the variation. This led me at once to a single word as the best *refrain*.

The question now arose as to the *character* of the word. Having made up my mind to a *refrain*, the division of the poem into stanzas was, of course, a corollary: the *refrain* forming the close to each stanza. That such a close, to have force, must be sonorous and susceptible of protracted emphasis, admitted no doubt: and these considerations inevitably led me to the long *o* as the most sonorous vowel, in connection with *r* as the most producible consonant.

The sound of the *refrain* being thus determined, it became necessary to select a word embodying this sound, and at the same time in the fullest possible keeping with that melancholy which I had pre-determined as the tone of the poem. In such a search it would have been absolutely impossible to overlook the word "Nevermore." In fact, it was the very first which presented itself.

The next *desideratum* was a pretext for the continuous use of the one word "nevermore." In observing the difficulty which I at once found in inventing a sufficiently plausible reason for its continuous repetition, I did not fail to perceive that this difficulty arose solely from the pre-assumption that the word was to be so continuously or monotonously spoken by *a human* being – I did not fail to perceive, in short, that the difficulty lay in the reconciliation of this monotony with the exercise of reason on the part of the creature repeating the word. Here, then, immediately arose the idea of a *non*-reasoning creature capable of speech; and, very naturally, a parrot, in the first instance, suggested itself, but was superseded forthwith by a Raven, as equally capable of speech, and infinitely more in keeping with the intended *tone*.

I had now gone so far as the conception of a Raven – the bird of ill omen – monotonously repeating the one word, "Nevermore," at the conclusion of each stanza, in a poem of melancholy tone, and in length about one hundred lines. Now, never losing sight of the object *supremeness*, or perfection, at all points, I asked myself – "Of all melancholy topics, what, according to the *universal* understanding of mankind, is the *most* melancholy?" Death – was the obvious reply. "And when," I said, "is this most melancholy of topics most poetical?" From what I have already explained at some length, the answer, here also, is obvious – "When it most closely allies itself to *Beauty*: the death, then, of a beautiful woman is, unquestionably, the most poetical topic in the world – and equally is it beyond doubt that the lips best suited for such topic are those of a bereaved lover."

I had now to combine the two ideas, of a lover lamenting his deceased mistress and a Raven continuously repeating the word "Nevermore" – I had to combine these, bearing in mind my design of varying, at every turn, the *application* of the word repeated; but the only intelligible mode of such combination is that of imagining the Raven employing the word in answer to the queries of the lover. And here it was that I saw at once the opportunity afforded for the effect on which I had been depending – that is to say, the effect of the *variation of application*. I saw that I could make the first query propounded by the lover – the first query to which the Raven should reply "Nevermore" – that I could make this first query a commonplace one – the second less so – the third still less, and so on – until at length the lover, startled from his original *nonchalance* by the melancholy character of the word itself – by its frequent repetition – and by a consideration of the ominous reputation of the fowl that uttered it – is at length excited to superstition, and wildly propounds queries of a far different character – queries whose solution he has passionately at heart – propounds them half in superstition and half in that species of despair which delights in self-torture – propounds them not altogether because he believes in the prophetic or demoniac character of the bird (which, reason assures him, is merely repeating a lesson learned by rote) but because he experiences a phrenzied pleasure in so modeling his questions as to receive from the *expected* "Nevermore" the most delicious because the most intolerable of sorrow. Perceiving the opportunity thus afforded me – or, more strictly, thus forced upon me in the progress of the construction – I first established in mind the climax, or concluding query – that to which "Nevermore" should be in the last place an answer – that in reply to which this word "Nevermore" should involve the utmost conceivable amount of sorrow and despair.

Here then the poem may be said to have its beginning – at the end, where all works of art should begin – for it was here, at this point of my preconsiderations, that I first put pen to paper in the composition of the stanza:

"Prophet," said I, "thing of evil! prophet still if bird or
    devil!
By that heaven that bends above us – by that God we
    both adore,
Tell this soul with sorrow laden, if within the distant
    Aidenn,

It shall clasp a sainted maiden whom the angels name
    Lenore –
Clasp a rare and radiant maiden whom the angels name
    Lenore."
            Quoth the raven "Nevermore."

I composed this stanza, at this point, first that, by establishing the climax, I might the better vary and graduate, as regards seriousness and importance, the preceding queries of the lover – and, secondly, that I might definitely settle the rhythm, the metre, and the length and general arrangement of the stanza – as well as graduate the stanzas which were to precede, so that none of them might surpass this in rhythmical effect. Had I been able, in the subsequent composition, to construct more vigorous stanzas, I should, without scruple, have purposely enfeebled them, so as not to interfere with the climacteric effect.

And here I may as well say a few words of the versification. My first object (as usual) was originality. The extent to which this has been neglected, in versification, is one of the most unaccountable things in the world. Admitting that there is little possibility of variety in mere *rhythm*, it is still clear that the possible varieties of metre and stanza are absolutely infinite – and yet, *for centuries, no man, in verse, has ever done, or ever seemed to think of doing, an original thing.* The fact is, originality (unless in minds of very unusual force) is by no means a matter, as some suppose, of impulse or intuition. In general, to be found, it must be elaborately sought, and although a positive merit of the highest class, demands in its attainment less of invention than negation.

Of course, I pretend to no originality in either the rhythm or metre of the "Raven." The former is trochaic – the latter is octameter acatalectic, alternating with heptameter catalectic repeated in the *refrain* of the fifth verse, and terminating with tetrameter catalectic. Less pedantically – the feet employed throughout (trochees) consist of a long syllable followed by a short: the first line of the stanza consists of eight of these feet – the second of seven and a half (in effect two-thirds) – the third of eight – the fourth of seven and a half – the fifth the same – the sixth three and a half. Now, each of these lines, taken individually, has been employed before, and what originality the "Raven" has, is in their *combination into stanza*; nothing even remotely approaching this combination has ever been attempted. The effect of this originality of combination is aided by other unusual, and some altogether novel effects, arising from an extension of the application of the principles of rhyme and alliteration.

The next point to be considered was the mode of bringing together the lover and the Raven – and the first branch of this consideration was the *locale.* For this the most natural suggestion might seem to be a forest, or the fields – but it has always appeared to me that a close *circumscription of space* is absolutely necessary to the effect of insulated incident: – it has the force of a frame to a picture. It has an indisputable moral power in keeping concentrated the attention, and, of course, must not be confounded with mere unity of place.

I determined, then, to place the lover in his chamber – in a chamber rendered sacred to him by memories of her who had frequented it. The room is represented as richly furnished – this in mere pursuance of the ideas I have already explained on the subject of Beauty, as the sole true poetical thesis.

The *locale* being thus determined, I had now to introduce the bird – and the thought of introducing him through the window, was inevitable. The idea of making the lover suppose, in the first instance, that the flapping of the wings of the bird against the shutter, is a "tapping" at the door, originated in a wish to increase, by prolonging, the reader's curiosity, and in a desire to admit the incidental effect arising from the lover's throwing open the door, finding all dark, and thence adopting the half-fancy that it was the spirit of his mistress that knocked.

I made the night tempestuous, first, to account for the Raven's seeking admission, and secondly, for the effect of contrast with the (physical) serenity within the chamber.

I made the bird alight on the bust of Pallas, also for the effect of contrast between the marble and the plumage – it being understood that the bust was absolutely *suggested* by the bird – the bust of *Pallas* being chosen, first, as most in keeping with the scholarship of the lover, and, secondly, for the sonorousness of the word, Pallas, itself.

About the middle of the poem, also, I have availed myself of the force of contrast, with a view of deepening the ultimate impression. For example, an air of the fantastic – approaching as nearly to the ludicrous as was admissible – is given to the Raven's entrance. He comes in "with many a flirt and flutter."

Not the *least obeisance made he* – not a moment stopped
  or stayed he,
But with mien of lord or lady, perched above my chamber
  door.

In the two stanzas which follow, the design is more obviously carried out: –

Then this ebony bird beguiling my sad fancy into
  smiling
By the *grave and stern decorum of the countenance it wore,*

"Though thy *crest be shorn and shaven* thou," I said, "art
   sure no craven,
Ghastly grim and ancient Raven wandering from the
   nightly shore –
Tell me what thy lordly name is on the Night's
   Plutonian shore!"
         Quoth the Raven "Nevermore."

Much I marvelled *this ungainly fowl* to hear discourse
   so plainly,
Though its answer little meaning – little relevancy
   bore;
For we cannot help agreeing that no living human
   being
*Ever yet was blessed with seeing bird above his chamber
   door* –
*Bird or beast upon the sculptured bust above his chamber
   door,*
         With such name as "Nevermore."

The effect of the *dénouement* being thus provided for, I
immediately drop the fantastic for a tone of the most
profound seriousness: – this tone commencing in the
stanza directly following the one last quoted, with the
line,

But the Raven, sitting lonely on that placid bust, spoke
only, etc.

From this epoch the lover no longer jests – no longer
sees any thing even of the fantastic in the Raven's
demeanor. He speaks of him as a "grim, ungainly,
ghastly, gaunt, and ominous bird of yore," and feels the
"fiery eyes" burning into his "bosom's core." This
revolution of thought, or fancy, on the lover's part, is
intended to induce a similar one on the part of the
reader – to bring the mind into a proper frame for the
dénouement – which is now brought about as rapidly and
as *directly* as possible.

With the *dénouement* proper – with the Raven's reply,
"Nevermore," to the lover's final demand if he shall
meet his mistress in another world – the poem, in its
obvious phase, that of a simple narrative, may be said to
have its completion. So far, every thing is within the
limits of the accountable – of the real. A raven, having
learned by rote the single word "Nevermore," and
having escaped from the custody of its owner, is driven,
at midnight, through the violence of a storm, to seek
admission at a window from which a light still gleams –
the chamber-window of a student, occupied half in
poring over a volume, half in dreaming of a beloved
mistress deceased. The casement being thrown open at
the fluttering of the bird's wings, the bird itself perches

on the most convenient seat out of the immediate reach of the student, who, amused by the incident and the oddity of the visiter's demeanor, demands of it, in jest and without looking for a reply, its name. The raven addressed, answers with its customary word, "Nevermore" – a word which finds immediate echo in the melancholy heart of the student, who, giving utterance aloud to certain thoughts suggested by the occasion, is again startled by the fowl's repetition of "Nevermore." The student now guesses the state of the case, but is impelled, as I have before explained, by the human thirst for self-torture, and in part by superstition, to propound such queries to the bird as will bring him, the lover, the most of the luxury of sorrow, through the anticipated answer "Nevermore." With the indulgence, to the utmost extreme, of this self-torture, the narration, in what I have termed its first or obvious phase, has a natural termination, and so far there has been no overstepping of the limits of the real.

But in subjects so handled, however skilfully, or with however vivid an array of incident, there is always a certain hardness or nakedness, which repels the artistical eye. Two things are invariably required – first, some amount of complexity, or more properly, adaptation; and, secondly, some amount of suggestiveness – some under current, however indefinite of meaning. It is this latter, in especial, which imparts to a work of art

179

so much of that *richness* (to borrow from colloquy a forcible term) which we are too fond of confounding with *the ideal*. It is the *excess* of the suggested meaning – it is the rendering this the upper instead of the under current of the theme – which turns into prose (and that of the very flattest kind) the so called poetry of the so called transcendentalists.

Holding these opinions, I added the two concluding stanzas of the poem – their suggestiveness being thus made to pervade all the narrative which has preceded them. The under current of meaning is rendered first apparent in the lines –

"Take thy beak from out *my heart*, and take thy form
   from off my door!"
       Quoth the Raven "Nevermore!"

It will be observed that the words, "from out my heart," involve the first metaphorical expression in the poem. They, with the answer, "Nevermore," dispose the mind to seek a moral in all that has been previously narrated. The reader begins now to regard the Raven as emblematical – but it is not until the very last line of the very last stanza, that the intention of making him emblematical of *Mournful and Never-ending Remembrance* is permitted distinctly to be seen:

And the Raven, never flitting, still is sitting, still is
   sitting,
On the pallid bust of Pallas just above my chamber
   door;
And his eyes have all the seeming of a demon's that is
   dreaming,
And the lamplight o'er him streaming throws his
   shadow on the floor;
And my soul *from out that shadow* that lies floating on
   the floor
        Shall be lifted – nevermore.

Graham's Magazine, April 1846

From THE POETIC PRINCIPLE

In speaking of the Poetic Principle, I have no design to be either thorough or profound. While discussing, very much at random, the essentiality of what we call Poetry, my principal purpose will be to cite for consideration, some few of those minor English or American poems which best suit my own taste, or which, upon my own fancy, have left the most definite impression. By "minor poems" I mean, of course, poems of little length. And here, in the beginning, permit me to say a few words in regard to a somewhat peculiar principle, which, whether rightfully or wrongfully, has always had its influence in my own critical estimate of the poem. I hold that a long poem does not exist. I maintain that the phrase, "a long poem," is simply a flat contradiction in terms.

I need scarcely observe that a poem deserves its title only inasmuch as it excites, by elevating the soul. The value of the poem is in the ratio of this elevating excitement. But all excitements are, through a psychal necessity, transient. That degree of excitement which would entitle a poem to be so called at all, cannot be sustained throughout a composition of any great length. After the lapse of half an hour, at the very utmost, it flags – fails – a revulsion ensues – and then the poem is, in effect, and in fact, no longer such.

There are, no doubt, many who have found difficulty in reconciling the critical dictum that the "Paradise Lost" is to be devoutly admired throughout, with the absolute impossibility of maintaining for it, during perusal, the amount of enthusiasm which that critical dictum would demand. This great work, in fact, is to be regarded as poetical, only when, losing sight of that vital requisite in all works of Art, Unity, we view it merely as a series of minor poems. If, to preserve its Unity – its totality of effect or impression – we read it (as would be necessary) at a single sitting, the result is but a constant alternation of excitement and depression. After a passage of what we feel to be true poetry, there follows, inevitably, a passage of platitude which no critical pre-judgment can force us to admire; but if, upon completing the work, we read it again, omitting the first book – that is to say, commencing with the second – we shall be surprised at now finding that admirable which we before condemned – that damnable which we had previously so much admired. It follows from all this that the ultimate, aggregate, or absolute effect of even the best epic under the sun, is a nullity: – and this is precisely the fact.

In regard to the Iliad, we have, if not positive proof, at least very good reason for believing it intended as a series of lyrics; but, granting the epic intention, I can say only that the work is based in an imperfect sense of art. The modern epic is, of the supposititious ancient model, but an inconsiderate and blindfold imitation. But the day of these artistic anomalies is over. If, at any time, any very long poem *were* popular in reality, which I doubt, it is at least clear that no very long poem will ever be popular again.

That the extent of a poetical work is, *cæteris paribus*, the measure of its merit, seems undoubtedly, when we thus state it, a proposition sufficiently absurd – yet we are indebted for it to the Quarterly Reviews. Surely there can be nothing in mere *size*, abstractly considered – there can be nothing in mere *bulk*, so far as a volume is concerned, which has so continuously elicited admiration from these saturnine pamphlets! A mountain, to be sure, by the mere sentiment of physical magnitude which it conveys, *does* impress us with a sense of the sublime – but no man is impressed after *this* fashion by the material grandeur of even "The Columbiad." Even the Quarterlies have not instructed us to be so impressed by it. *As yet*, they have not *insisted* on our estimating Lamartine by the cubic foot, or Pollock by the pound – but what else are we to *infer* from their continual prating about "sustained effort?" If, by "sustained effort," any little gentleman has accomplished an epic, let us frankly commend him for the effort – if this indeed be a thing commendable – but let us forbear praising the epic on the effort's account. It is to be hoped that common sense, in the time to come, will prefer deciding upon a work of art, rather by the impression it makes, by the effect it produces, than by the time it took to impress the effect, or by the amount of "sustained effort" which had been found necessary in effecting the impression. The fact is, that perseverance is one thing, and genius quite another; nor can all the Quarterlies in Christendom confound them. By and by, this proposition, with many which I have been just urging, will be received as self-evident. In the mean time, by being generally condemned as falsities, they will not be essentially damaged as truths.

On the other hand, it is clear that a poem may be improperly brief. Undue brevity degenerates into mere epigrammatism. A *very* short poem, while now and then producing a brilliant or vivid, never produces a profound or enduring effect. There must be the steady pressing down of the stamp upon the wax. De Béranger has wrought innumerable things, pungent and spirit-stirring; but, in general, they have been too imponderous to stamp themselves deeply into the public attention; and thus, as so many feathers of fancy, have been blown aloft only to be whistled down the wind.

A remarkable instance of the effect of undue brevity in depressing a poem – in keeping it out of the popular view – is afforded by the following exquisite little Serenade.

I arise from dreams of thee,
    In the first sweet sleep of night,
When the winds are breathing low,
    And the stars are shining bright.
I arise from dreams of thee,
    And a spirit in my feet
Has led me – who knows how? –
    To thy chamber-window, sweet!

The wandering airs they faint
    On the dark, the silent stream –
The champak odours fail
    Like sweet thoughts in a dream;
The nightingale's complaint,
    It dies upon her heart
As I must die on thine,
    O, beloved as thou art!

O, lift me from the grass!
    I die, I faint, I fail!
Let thy love in kisses rain
    On my lips and eyelids pale.
My cheek is cold and white, alas!
    My heart beats loud and fast:
Oh! press it close to thine again,
    Where it will break at last!

Very few, perhaps, are familiar with these lines – yet no less a poet than Shelley is their author. Their warm, yet delicate and ethereal imagination will be appreciated by all – but by none so thoroughly as by him who has himself arisen from sweet dreams of one beloved, to bathe in the aromatic air of a southern mid-summer night.

One of the finest poems by Willis – the very best, in my opinion, which he has ever written – has, no doubt, through the same defect of undue brevity, been kept back from its proper position, not less in the critical than in the popular view.

> The shadows lay along Broadway,
>   'Twas near the twilight-tide –
> And slowly there a lady fair
>   Was walking in her pride.
> Alone walked she; but, viewlessly,
>   Walked spirits at her side.
>
> Peace charmed the street beneath her feet,
>   And Honour charmed the air;
> And all astir looked kind on her,
>   And called her good as fair –
> For all God ever gave to her
>   She kept with chary care.

She kept with care her beauties rare
    From lovers warm and true –
For her heart was cold to all but gold,
    And the rich came not to woo –
But honoured well are charms to sell
    If priests the selling do.

Now walking there was one more fair –
    A slight girl, lily-pale;
And she had unseen company
    To make the spirit quail –
'Twixt Want and Scorn she walked forlorn,
    And nothing could avail.

No mercy now can clear her brow
    For this world's peace to pray;
For, as love's wild prayer dissolved in air,
    Her woman's heart gave way! –
But the sin forgiven by Christ in Heaven
    By man is cursed alway!

In this composition we find it difficult to recognise the Willis who has written so many mere "verses of society." The lines are not only richly ideal, but full of energy; while they breathe an earnestness – an evident sincerity of sentiment – for which we look in vain throughout all the other works of this author.

While the epic mania – while the idea that, to merit in poetry, prolixity is indispensable – has, for some years past, been gradually dying out of the public mind, by mere dint of its own absurdity – we find it succeeded by a heresy too palpably false to be long tolerated, but one which, in the brief period it has already endured, may be said to have accomplished more in the corruption of our Poetical Literature than all its other enemies combined. I allude to the heresy of *The Didactic*. It has been assumed, tacitly and avowedly, directly and indirectly, that the ultimate object of all Poetry is Truth. Every poem, it is said, should inculcate a moral; and by this moral is the poetical merit of the work to be adjudged. We Americans, especially, have patronised this happy idea; and we Bostonians, very especially, have developed it in full. We have taken it into our heads that to write a poem simply for the poem's sake, and to acknowledge such to have been our design, would be to confess ourselves radically wanting in the true Poetic dignity and force: – but the simple fact is, that, would we but permit ourselves to look into our own souls, we should immediately there discover that under the sun there neither exists nor *can* exist any work more thoroughly dignified – more supremely noble than this very poem – this poem *per se* – this poem which is a poem and nothing more – this poem written solely for the poem's sake.

With as deep a reverence for the True as ever inspired the bosom of man, I would, nevertheless, limit, in some measure, its modes of inculcation. I would limit to enforce them. I would not enfeeble them by dissipation. The demands of Truth are severe. She has no sympathy with the myrtles. All *that* which is so indispensable in Song, is precisely all *that* with which *she* has nothing whatever to do. It is but making her a flaunting paradox, to wreathe her in gems and flowers. In enforcing a truth, we need severity rather than efflorescence of language. We must be simple, precise, terse. We must be cool, calm, unimpassioned. In a word, we must be in that mood which, as nearly as possible, is the exact converse of the poetical. *He* must be blind, indeed, who does not perceive the radical and chasmal differences between the truthful and the poetical modes of inculcation. He must be theory-mad beyond redemption who, in spite of these differences, shall still persist in attempting to reconcile the obstinate oils and waters of Poetry and Truth.

Dividing the world of mind into its three most immediately obvious distinctions, we have the Pure Intellect, Taste, and the Moral Sense. I place Taste in the middle, because it is just this position, which, in the mind, it occupies. It holds intimate relations with either extreme; but from the Moral Sense is separated by so faint a difference that Aristotle has not hesitated to place some of its operations among the virtues themselves. Nevertheless, we find the *offices* of the trio marked with a sufficient distinction. Just as the Intellect concerns itself with Truth, so Taste informs us of the Beautiful while the Moral Sense is regardful of Duty. Of this latter, while Conscience teaches the obligation, and Reason the expediency, Taste contents herself with displaying the charms: – waging war upon Vice solely on the ground of her deformity – her disproportion – her animosity to the fitting, to the appropriate, to the harmonious – in a word, to Beauty.

An immortal instinct, deep within the spirit of man, is thus, plainly, a sense of the Beautiful. This it is which administers to his delight in the manifold forms, and sounds, and odours, and sentiments amid which he exists. And just as the lily is repeated in the lake, or the eyes of Amaryllis in the mirror, so is the mere oral or written repetition of these forms, and sounds, and colours, and odours, and sentiments, a duplicate source of delight. But this mere repetition is not poetry. He who shall simply sing, with however glowing enthusiasm, or with however vivid a truth of description, of the sights, and sounds, and odours, and colours, and sentiments, which greet *him* in common with all mankind – he, I say, has yet failed to prove his divine title. There is still a something in the distance which he has been unable to attain. We have still a thirst unquenchable, to allay which he has not shown us the crystal springs. This thirst belongs to the immortality of Man. It is at once a consequence and an indication of his perennial existence. It is the desire of the moth for the star. It is no mere appreciation of the Beauty before us – but a wild effort to reach the Beauty above. Inspired by an ecstatic prescience of the glories beyond the grave, we struggle, by multiform combinations among the things and thoughts of Time, to attain a portion of that Loveliness whose very elements, perhaps, appertain to eternity alone. And thus when by Poetry – or when by Music, the most entrancing of the Poetic moods – we find ourselves melted into tears – we weep then – not as the Abaté Gravina supposes – through excess of pleasure, but through a certain, petulant, impatient sorrow at our inability to grasp *now*, wholly, here on earth, at once and for ever, those divine and rapturous joys, of which *through* the poem, or *through* the music, we attain to but brief and indeterminate glimpses.

The struggle to apprehend the supernal Loveliness – this struggle, on the part of souls fittingly constituted – has given to the world all *that* which it (the world) has ever been enabled at once to understand and *to feel* as poetic.

The Poetic Sentiment, of course, may develope itself in various modes – in Painting, in Sculpture, in Architecture, in the Dance – very especially in Music – and very peculiarly, and with a wide field, in the composition of the Landscape Garden. Our present theme, however, has regard only to its manifestation in words. And here let me speak briefly on the topic of rhythm. Contenting myself with the certainty that Music, in its various modes of metre, rhythm, and rhyme, is of so vast a moment in Poetry as never to be wisely rejected – is so vitally important an adjunct, that he is simply silly who declines its assistance, I will not now pause to maintain its absolute essentiality. It is in Music, perhaps, that the soul most nearly attains the great end for which, when inspired with the Poetic Sentiment, it struggles – the creation of supernal Beauty. It *may* be, indeed, that here this sublime end is, now and then, attained *in fact.* We are often made to feel, with a shivering delight, that from an earthly harp are stricken notes which *cannot* have been unfamiliar to the angels. And thus there can be little doubt that in the union of Poetry with Music in its popular sense, we shall find the widest field for the Poetic development. The old Bards and Minnesingers had advantages which we do not possess – and Thomas Moore, singing his own songs, was, in the most legitimate manner, perfecting them as poems.

To recapitulate, then: – I would define, in brief, the Poetry of words as *The Rhythmical Creation of Beauty*.

Its sole arbiter is Taste. With the Intellect or with the Conscience, it has only collateral relations. Unless incidentally, it has no concern whatever either with Duty or with Truth.

A few words, however, in explanation. *That* pleasure which is at once the most pure, the most elevating, and the most intense, is derived, I maintain, from the contemplation of the Beautiful. In the contemplation of Beauty we alone find it possible to attain that pleasurable elevation, or excitement, *of the soul*, which we recognise as the Poetic Sentiment, and which is so easily distinguished from Truth, which is the satisfaction of the Reason, or from Passion, which is the excitement of the heart. I make Beauty, therefore – using the word as inclusive of the sublime – I make Beauty the province of the poem, simply because it is an obvious rule of Art that effects should be made to spring as directly as possible from their causes: – no one as yet having been weak enough to deny that the peculiar elevation in question is at least *most readily* attainable in the poem. It by no means follows, however, that the incitements of Passion, or the precepts of Duty, or even the lessons of Truth, may not be introduced into a poem, and with advantage; for they may subserve, incidentally, in various ways, the general purposes of the work: – but the true artist will always contrive to tone them down in proper subjection to that *Beauty* which is the atmosphere and the real essence of the poem.

Thus, although in a very cursory and imperfect manner, I have endeavoured to convey to you my conception of the Poetic Principle. It has been my purpose to suggest that, while this Principle itself is, strictly and simply, the Human Aspiration for Supernal Beauty, the manifestation of the Principle is always found in *an elevating excitement of the Soul* – quite independent of that passion which is the intoxication of the Heart – or of that Truth which is the satisfaction of the Reason. For, in regard to Passion, alas! its tendency is to degrade, rather than to elevate the Soul. Love, on the contrary – Love – the true, the divine Eros – the Uranian, as distinguished from the Dionæan Venus – is unquestionably the purest and truest of all poetical themes. And in regard to Truth – if, to be sure, through the attainment of a truth, we are led to perceive a harmony where none was apparent before, we experience, at once, the true poetical effect – but this effect is referable to the harmony alone, and not in the least degree to the truth which merely served to render the harmony manifest.

We shall reach, however, more immediately a distinct conception of what the true Poetry is, by mere reference to a few of the simple elements which induce in the Poet himself the true poetical effect. He recognises the ambrosia which nourishes his soul, in the bright orbs that shine in Heaven – in the volutes of the flower – in the clustering of low shrubberies – in the waving of the grain-fields – in the slanting of tall, Eastern trees – in the blue distance of mountains – in the grouping of clouds – in the twinkling of half-hidden brooks – in the gleaming of silver rivers – in the repose of sequestered lakes – in the star-mirroring depths of lonely wells. He perceives it in the songs of birds – in the harp of Æolus – in the sighing of the night-wind – in the repining voice of the forest – in the surf that complains to the shore – in the fresh breath of the woods – in the scent of the violet – in the voluptuous perfume of the hyacinth – in the suggestive odour that comes to him, at eventide, from far-distant, undiscovered islands, over dim oceans, illimitable and unexplored. He owns it in all noble thoughts – in all unworldly motives – in all holy impulses – in all chivalrous, generous, and self-sacrificing deeds. He feels it in the beauty of woman – in the grace of her step – in the lustre of her eye – in the melody of her voice – in her soft laughter – in her sigh – in the harmony of the rustling of her robes. He deeply feels it in her winning endearments – in her burning enthusiasms – in her gentle charities – in her meek and devotional endurances – but above all – ah, far above all – he kneels to it – he worships it in the faith, in the purity, in the strength, in the altogether divine majesty – of her *love.*

Let me conclude — by the recitation of yet another brief poem — one very different in character from any that I have before quoted. It is by Motherwell, and is called "The Song of the Cavalier." With our modern and altogether rational ideas of the absurdity and impiety of warfare, we are not precisely in that frame of mind best adapted to sympathize with the sentiments, and thus to appreciate the real excellence of the poem. To do this fully, we must identify ourselves, in fancy, with the soul of the old cavalier.

> Then mounte! then mounte, brave gallants, all,
>   And don your helmes amaine:
> Deathe's couriers, Fame and Honour, call
>   Us to the field againe.
>
> No shrewish teares shall fill our eye
>   When the sword-hilt is in our hand, —
> Heart-whole we'll part, and no whit sighe
>   For the fayrest of the land;
> Let piping swaine, and craven wight,
>   Thus weepe and puling crye,
> Our business is like men to fight,
>   And hero-like to die!

Sartain's Union Magazine, October 1850

From THE RATIONALE OF VERSE

Verse originates in the human enjoyment of equality, fitness. To this enjoyment, also, all the moods of verse – rhythm, metre, stanza, rhyme, alliteration, the *refrain*, and other analogous effects – are to be referred. As there are some readers who habitually confound rhythm and metre, it may be as well here to say that the former concerns the *character* of feet (that is, the arrangements of syllables) while the latter has to do with the *number* of these feet. Thus by "a dactylic *rhythm*" we express a sequence of dactyls. By "a dactylic hexa*meter*" we imply a line or measure consisting of six of these dactyls.

To return to *equality*. Its idea embraces those of similarity, proportion, identity, repetition, and adapt-ation or fitness. It might not be very difficult to go even behind the idea of equality, and show both how and why it is that the human nature takes pleasure in it, but such an investigation would, for any purpose now in view, be supererogatory. It is sufficient that the *fact* is undeni-able – the fact that man derives enjoyment from his perception of equality. Let us examine a crystal. We are at once interested by the equality between the sides and between the angles of one of its faces: the equality of the sides pleases us; that of the angles doubles the pleasure. On bringing to view a second face in all respects similar to the first, this pleasure seems to be squared; on bringing to view a third it appears to be cubed, and so on. I have no doubt, indeed, that the delight experienced, if measurable, would be found to have exact mathematical relations such as I suggest; that is to say, as far as a certain point, beyond which there would be a decrease in similar relations.

The perception of pleasure in the equality of *sounds* is the principle of *Music*. Unpractised ears can appreciate only simple equalities, such as are found in ballad airs. While comparing one simple sound with another they are too much occupied to be capable of comparing the equality subsisting between these two simple sounds, taken conjointly, and two other similar simple sounds taken conjointly. Practised ears, on the other hand, appreciate both equalities at the same instant – although it is absurd to suppose that both are *heard* at the same instant. One is heard and appreciated from itself: the other is heard by the memory; and the instant glides into and is confounded with the secondary, appreciation. Highly cultivated musical taste in this manner enjoys not only these double equalities, all appreciated at once, but takes pleasurable cognizance, through memory, of equalities the members of which occur at intervals so great that the uncultivated taste loses them altogether. That this latter can properly estimate or decide on the merits of what is called scientific music, is of course impossible. But scientific music has no claim to intrinsic excellence – it is fit for scientific ears alone. In its excess it is the triumph of the *physique* over the *morale* of music. The sentiment is overwhelmed by the sense. On the whole, the advocates of the simpler melody and harmony have infinitely the best of the argument; – although there has been very little of real argument on the subject.

In *verse*, which cannot be better designated than as an inferior or less capable Music, there is, happily, little chance for complexity. Its rigidly simple character not even Science – not even Pedantry can greatly pervert.

The rudiment of verse may, possibly, be found in the *spondee.* The very germ of a thought seeking satisfaction in equality of sound, would result in the construction of words of two syllables, equally accented. In corroboration of this idea we find that spondees most abound in the most ancient tongues. The second step we can easily suppose to be the comparison, that is to say, the collocation, of two spondees – of two words composed each of a spondee. The third step would be the juxtaposition of three of these words. By this time the perception of monotone would induce farther consideration: and thus arises what Leigh Hunt so flounders in discussing under the title of "The *Principle* of Variety in Uniformity." Of course there is no principle in the case – nor in maintaining it. The "Uniformity" is the principle:

– the "Variety" is but the principle's natural safeguard from self-destruction by excess of self. "Uniformity," besides, is the very worst word that could have been chosen for the expression of the *general* idea at which it aims.

The perception of monotone having given rise to an attempt at its relief, the first thought in this new direction would be that of collating two or more words formed each of two syllables differently accented (that is to say, short and long) but having the same order in each word: – in other terms, of collating two or more iambuses, or two or more trochees. And here let me pause to assert that more pitiable nonsense has been written on the topic of *long* and *short* syllables than on any other subject under the sun. In general, a syllable is long or short, just as it is difficult or easy of enunciation. The *natural* long syllables are those encumbered – the *natural* short ones are those *un*encumbered, with consonants; all the rest is mere artificiality and jargon. The Latin Prosodies have a rule that "a vowel before two consonants is long." This rule is deduced from "authority" – that is, from the observation that vowels so circumstanced, in the ancient poems, are always in syllables long by the laws of scansion. The philosophy of the rule is untouched, and lies simply in the physical difficulty of giving voice to such syllables – of performing the lingual evolutions necessary for their utterance. Of course, it is not the *vowel* that is long (although the rule says so) but the syllable of which the vowel is a part. It will be seen that the length of a syllable, depending on the facility or difficulty of its enunciation, must have great variation in various syllables; but for the purposes of verse we suppose a long syllable equal to two short ones: – and the natural deviation from this relativeness we correct in perusal. The more closely our long syllables approach this relation with our short ones, the better, *ceteris paribus,* will be our verse: but if the relation does not exist of itself, we force it by emphasis, which can, of course, make any syllable as long as desired; – or, by an effort we can pronounce with unnatural brevity a syllable that is naturally too long. *Accented* syllables are of course always long – but, where *un*encumbered with consonants, must be classed among the *unnaturally* long. Mere custom has declared that we shall accent them – that is to say, dwell upon them; but no inevitable lingual difficulty forces us to do so. In fine, every long syllable must of its own accord occupy in its utterance, or must be *made* to occupy, precisely the time demanded for two short ones. The only exception to this rule is found in the cæsura – of which more anon.

The success of the experiment with the trochees or iambuses (the one would have suggested the other) must have led to a trial of dactyls or anapæsts – natural dactyls or anapæsts – dactylic or anapæstic *words*. And now some degree of complexity has been attained. There is an appreciation, first, of the equality between the several dactyls, or anapæsts, and, secondly, of that between the long syllable and the two short conjointly. But here it may be said that step after step would have been taken, in continuation of this routine, until all the feet of the Greek Prosodies became exhausted. Not so: – these remaining feet have no existence except in the brains of the scholiasts. It is needless to imagine men inventing these things, and folly to explain how and why they invented them, until it shall be first shown that they are actually invented. All other "feet" than those which I have specified, are, if not impossible at first view, merely combinations of the specified; and, although this assertion is rigidly true, I will, to avoid misunderstanding, put it in a somewhat different shape. I will say, then, that at present I am aware of no *rhythm* – nor do I believe that any one can be constructed – which, in its last analysis, will not be found to consist altogether of the feet I have mentioned, either existing in their individual and obvious condition, or interwoven with each other in accordance with simple natural laws which I will endeavor to point out hereafter.

We have now gone so far as to suppose men constructing indefinite sequences of spondaic, iambic, trochaic, dactylic, or anapæstic words. In *extending* these sequences, they would be again arrested by the sense of monotone. A succession of spondees would *immediately* have displeased; one of iambuses or of trochees, on account of the variety included within the foot itself, would have taken longer to displease; one of dactyls or anapæsts still longer: but even the last if extended very far, must have become wearisome. The idea, first, of curtailing, and secondly, of defining the length of a sequence, would thus at once have arisen. Here then is the *line*, or verse proper.[1] The principle of equality being constantly at the bottom of the whole process, lines would naturally be made, in the first instance, equal in the number of their feet; in the second instance there would be variation in the mere number; one line would be twice as long as another; then one would be some less obvious multiple of another; then still less obvious proportions would be adopted: – nevertheless there would be *proportion*, that is to say a phase of equality, still.

1 Verse, from the Latin *vertere*, to turn, is so called on account of the turning or recommencement of the series of feet. Thus a verse, strictly speaking, is a line. In this sense, however, I have preferred using the latter word alone; employing the former in the general acceptation given it in the heading of this paper.

Lines being once introduced, the necessity of distinctly defining these lines *to the ear*, (as yet written verse does not exist,) would lead to a scrutiny of their capabilities *at their terminations*: — and now would spring up the idea of equality in sound between the final syllables — in other words, of *rhyme*. First, it would be used only in the iambic, anapæstic, and spondaic rhythms, (granting that the latter had not been thrown aside, long since, on account of its tameness;) because in these rhythms the concluding syllable, being long, could best sustain the necessary protraction of the voice. No great while could elapse, however, before the effect, found pleasant as well as useful, would be applied to the two remaining rhythms. But as the chief force of rhyme must lie in the accented syllable, the attempt to create rhyme at all in these two remaining rhythms, the trochaic and dactylic, would necessarily result in double and triple rhymes, such as *beauty* with *duty* (trochaic) and *beautiful* with *dutiful* (dactylic.)

It must be observed that in suggesting these processes I assign them no date; nor do I even insist upon their order. Rhyme is supposed to be of modern origin, and were this proved, my positions remain untouched. I may say, however, in passing, that several instances of rhyme occur in the "Clouds" of Aristophanes, and that the Roman poets occasionally employ it. There is an effective species of ancient rhyming which has never descended to the moderns; that in which the ultimate and penultimate syllables rhyme with each other. For example:

Parturiunt montes et nascitur ridicu*lus mus*.

and again –

Litoreis ingens inventa sub ilici*bus sus*.

The terminations of Hebrew verse, (as far as understood,) show no signs of rhyme; but what thinking person can doubt that it did actually exist? That men have so obstinately and blindly insisted, *in general*, even up to the present day, in confining rhyme to the *ends* of lines, when its effect is even better applicable elsewhere, intimates, in my opinion, the sense of some *necessity* in the connexion of the end with the rhyme – hints that the origin of rhyme lay in a necessity which connected it with the end – shows that neither mere accident nor mere fancy gave rise to the connexion – points, in a word, at the very necessity which I have suggested, (that of some mode of defining lines *to the ear*,) as the true origin of rhyme. Admit this and we throw the origin far back in the night of Time – beyond the origin of written verse.

But to resume. The amount of complexity I have now supposed to be attained is very considerable. Various systems of equalization are appreciated at once (or nearly so) in their respective values and in the value of each system with reference to all the others. As our present *ultimatum* of complexity we have arrived at triple-rhymed, natural-dactylic lines, existing proportionally as well as equally with regard to other triple-rhymed, natural-dactylic lines. For example:

> Virginal Lilian, rigidly, humblily dutiful;
> Saintlily, lowlily,
> Thrillingly, holily
> Beautiful!

Here we appreciate, first, the absolute equality between the long syllable of each dactyl and the two short conjointly; secondly, the absolute equality between each dactyl and any other dactyl – in other words, among all the dactyls; thirdly, the absolute equality between the two middle lines; fourthly, the absolute equality between the first line and all the others taken conjointly; fifthly, the absolute equality between the two last syllables of the respective words "dutiful" and "beautiful;" sixthly, the absolute equality between the two last syllables of the respective words "lowlily" and "holily;" seventhly, the proximate equality between the first syllable of "dutiful" and the first syllable of "beautiful;" eighthly, the proximate equality between the first syllable of "lowlily" and that of "holily;" ninthly, the proportional equality, (that of five to one,) between the first line and each of its members, the dactyls; tenthly, the proportional equality, (that of two to one,) between each of the middle lines and its members, the dactyls; eleventhly, the proportional equality between the first line and each of the two middle – that of five to two; twelfthly, the proportional equality between the first line and the last – that of five to one; thirteenthly, the proportional equality between each of the middle lines and the last – that of two to one; lastly, the proportional equality, as concerns number, between all the lines, taken collectively, and any individual line – that of four to one.

The consideration of this last equality would give birth immediately to the idea of *stanza*[2] – that is to say, the insulation of lines into equal or obviously proportional masses. In its primitive, (which was also its best,) form, the stanza would most probably have had absolute unity. In other words, the removal of any one of its lines would have rendered it imperfect; as in the case above, where if the last line, for example, be taken away, there is left no rhyme to the "dutiful" of the first. Modern stanza is excessively loose, and where so, ineffective as a matter of course.

2 A stanza is often vulgarly, and with gross impropriety, called a *verse*.

Now, although in the deliberate written statement which I have here given of these various systems of equalities, there seems to be an infinity of complexity – so much that it is hard to conceive the mind taking cognizance of them all in the brief period occupied by the perusal or recital of the stanza – yet the difficulty is in fact apparent only when we will it to become so. Any one fond of mental experiment may satisfy himself, by trial, that, in listening to the lines, he does actually, (although with a seeming unconsciousness, on account of the rapid evolutions of sensation,) recognize and instantaneously appreciate, (more or less intensely as his ear is cultivated,) each and all of the equalizations detailed. The pleasure received, or receivable, has very much such progressive increase, and in very nearly such mathematical relations, as those which I have suggested in the case of the crystal.

It will be observed that I speak of merely a proximate equality between the first syllable of "dutiful" and that of "beautiful;" and it may be asked why we cannot imagine the earliest rhymes to have had absolute instead of proximate equality of sound. But absolute equality would have involved the use of identical words; and it is the duplicate sameness or monotony – that of sense as well as that of sound – which would have caused these rhymes to be rejected in the very first instance.

The narrowness of the limits within which verse composed of natural feet alone, must necessarily have been confined, would have led, after a *very* brief interval, to the trial and immediate adoption of artifical feet – that is to say of feet *not* constituted each of a single word, but two or even three words; or of parts of words. These feet would be intermingled with natural ones. For example:

ă brēath | căn māke | thĕm ās | ă brēath | hăs māde.

This is an iambic line in which each iambus is formed of two words. Again:

Thĕ ūn | ĭmā | gĭnā | blĕ mīght | ŏf Jōve. |

This is an iambic line in which the first foot is formed of a word and a part of a word; the second and third of parts taken from the body or interior of a word; the fourth of a part and a whole; the fifth of two complete words. There are no *natural* feet in either lines. Again:

Cān ĭt bĕ | fāncĭĕd thăt | Dēīty | ēvĕr vīn | dīctĭvely |
Māde ĭn hĭs | īmagĕ ă | mānnĭkĭn | mĕrely tŏ | māddĕn ĭt? |

These are two dactylic lines in which we find natural feet, ("Deity," "mannikin;") feet composed of two words ("fancied that," "image a," "merely to," "madden it;")

feet composed of three words ("can it be," "made in his;") a foot composed of a part of a word ("dictively;") and a foot composed of a word and a part of a word ("ever vin.")

And now, in our supposititious progress, we have gone so far as to exhaust all the *essentialities* of verse. What follows may, strictly speaking, be recorded as embellishment merely – but even in this embellishment, the rudimental sense of *equality* would have been the never-ceasing impulse. It would, for example, be simply in seeking farther administration to this sense that men would come, in time, to think of the *refrain*, or burden, where, at the closes of the several stanzas of a poem, one word or phrase is *repeated*; and of alliteration, in whose simplest form a consonant is *repeated* in the commencements of various words. This effect would be extended so as to embrace repetitions both of vowels and of consonants, in the bodies as well as in the beginnings of words; and, at a later period, would be made to infringe on the province of rhyme, by the introduction of general similarity of sound between whole feet occurring in the body of a line: – all of which modifications I have exemplified in the line above,

*M*ade in his i*m*age a *mannikin m*erely to *madden it.*

Farther cultivation would improve also the *refrain* by relieving its monotone in slightly varying the phrase at each repetition, or, (as I have attempted to do in "The Raven,") in retaining the phrase and varying its application – although this latter point is not strictly a rhythmical effect *alone*. Finally, poets when fairly wearied with following precedent – following it the more closely the less they perceived it in company with Reason – would adventure so far as to indulge in positive rhyme at other points than the ends of lines. First, they would put it in the middle of the line; then at some point where the multiple would be less obvious; then alarmed at their own audacity, they would undo all their work by cutting these lines in two. And here is the fruitful source of the infinity of "short metre," by which modern poetry, if not distinguished, is at least disgraced. It would require a high degree, indeed, both of cultivation and of courage, on the part of any versifier, to enable him to place his rhymes – and let them remain – at unquestionably their best position, that of unusual and *unanticipated* intervals.

On account of the stupidity of some people, or, (if talent be a more respectable word,) on account of their talent for misconception – I think it necessary to add here, first, that I believe the "processes" above detailed to be nearly if not accurately those which *did* occur in the gradual creation of what we now call verse; secondly, that, although I so believe, I yet urge neither the assumed fact nor my belief in it, as a part of the true proposition of this paper; thirdly, that in regard to the aim of this paper, it is of no consequence whether these processes did occur either in the order I have assigned them, or at all; my design being simply, in presenting a general type of what such processes *might* have been and *must* have resembled, to help *them*, the "some people," to an easy understanding of what I have farther to say on the topic of Verse.

I shall now best proceed in quoting the initial lines of Byron's "Bride of Abydos:"

Know ye the land where the cypress and myrtle
    Are emblems of deeds that are done in their clime –
Where the rage of the vulture, the love of the turtle
    Now melt into softness, now madden to crime?
Know ye the land of the cedar and vine,
Where the flowers ever blossom, the beams ever shine,
And the light wings of Zephyr, oppressed with perfume,
Wax faint o'er the gardens of Gul in their bloom?
Where the citron and olive are fairest of fruit
And the voice of the nightingale never is mute –
Where the virgins are soft as the roses they twine,
And all save the spirit of man is divine?
'Tis the land of the East – 'tis the land of the Sun –
Can he smile on such deeds as his children have done?
Oh, wild as the accents of lovers' farewell
Are the hearts that they bear and the tales that they tell.

Now the flow of these lines, (as times go,) is very sweet and musical. They have been often admired, and justly – as times go – that is to say, it is a rare thing to find better versification of its kind. And where verse is pleasant to the ear, it is silly to find fault with it because it refuses to be scanned. Yet I have heard men, professing to be scholars, who made no scruple of abusing these lines of Byron's on the ground that they were musical in spite of *all law*. Other gentlemen, *not* scholars, abused "all law" for the same reason: – and it occurred neither to the one party nor to the other that the law about which they were disputing might possibly be no law at all – an ass of a law in the skin of a lion.

The Grammars said something about dactylic lines, and it was easily seen that *these* lines were at least meant for dactylic. The first one was, therefore, thus divided:

Knōw yĕ thĕ | lānd whĕre thĕ | cyprĕss ănd | myrtle. |

The concluding foot was a mystery; but the Prosodies said something about the dactylic "measure" calling now and then for a double rhyme; and the court of enquiry were content to rest in the double rhyme, without exactly perceiving what a double rhyme had to do with the question of an irregular foot. Quitting the first line, the second was thus scanned:

Arē ĕmblĕms | ōf deĕds thăt | āre dŏne ĭn | thēir clĭme. |

It was immediately seen, however, that *this* would not do: – it was at war with the whole emphasis of the reading. It could not be supposed that Byron, or any one in his senses, intended to place stress upon such monosyllables as "are," "of," and "their," nor could "their clime," collated with "to crime," in the corresponding line below, be fairly twisted into anything like a "double rhyme," so as to bring everything within the category of the Grammars. But farther these Grammars spoke not. The inquirers, therefore, in spite of their sense of harmony in the lines, when considered without reference to scansion, fell back upon the idea that the "Are" was a blunder – an excess for which the poet should be sent to Coventry – and, striking it out, they scanned the remainder of the line as follows:

—ēmblĕms ōf | deĕds thăt ăre | dōne ĭn thēir | clĭme. |

This answered pretty well; but the Grammars admitted no such foot as a foot of one syllable; and besides the rhythm was dactylic. In despair, the books are well searched, however, and at last the investigators are gratified by a full solution of the riddle in the profound "Observation" quoted in the beginning of this article: –

"When a syllable is wanting, the verse is said to be catalectic; when the measure is exact, the line is acatalectic; when there is a redundant syllable it forms hypermeter." This is enough. The anomalous line is pronounced to be catalectic at the head and to form hypermeter at the tail: — and so on, and so on; it being soon discovered that nearly all the remaining lines are in a similar predicament, and that what flows so smoothly to the ear, although so roughly to the eye, is, after all, a mere jumble of catalecticism, acatalecticism, and hypermeter — not to say worse.

Now, had this court of inquiry been in possession of even the shadow of the *philosophy* of Verse, they would have had no trouble in reconciling this oil and water of the eye and ear, by merely scanning the passage without reference to lines, and, continuously, thus:

Know ye the | land where the | cypress and | myrtle
Are | emblems of | deeds that are | done in their | clime
Where the | rage of the | vulture the | love of the |
turtle Now | melt into | softness now | madden to |
crime | Know ye the | land of the | cedar and | vine
Where the | flowers ever | blossom the | beams ever |
shine Where the | light wings of | Zephyr op | pressed
by per | *fume Wax* | faint o'er the | gardens of | Gul in
their | bloom Where the | citron and | olive are | fairest
of | fruit And the | voice of the | nightingale | never is |

mute Where the | virgins are | soft as the | roses they |
twine And | all save the | spirit of | man is di | vine 'Tis
the | land of the | East 'tis the | clime of the | Sun Can
he | smile on such | deeds as his | children have | *done
Oh* | wild as the | accents of | lovers' fare | well Are the |
hearts that they | bear and the | tales that they | *tell.*

Here "crime" and "tell" (italicized) are cæsuras, each
having the value of a dactyl, four short syllables; while
"fume Wax," "twine and," and "done Oh," are spondees
which, of course, being composed of two long syllables,
are also equal to four short, and are the dactyl's natural
equivalent. The nicety of Byron's ear has led him into a
succession of feet which, with two trivial exceptions as
regards melody, are absolutely accurate – a very rare
occurrence this in dactylic or anapæstic rhythms. The
exceptions are found in the spondee *"twine And"* and
the dactyl, *"smile on such."* Both feet are false in point of
melody. In *"twine And,"* to make out the rhythm, we
must force *"And"* into a length which it will not
naturally bear. We are called on to sacrifice either the
proper length of the syllable as demanded by its
position as a member of a spondee, or the customary
accentuation of the word in conversation. There is no
hesitation, and should be none. We at once give up the
sound for the sense; and the rhythm is imperfect. In
this instance it is *very* slightly so; – not one person in

ten thousand could, by ear, detect the inaccuracy. But the *perfection* of verse, as regards melody, consists in its *never* demanding any such sacrifice as is here demanded. The rhythmical must agree, *thoroughly*, with the reading flow. This perfection has in no instance been attained – but is unquestionably attainable. *"Smile on such,"* the dactyl, is incorrect, because *"such,"* from the character of the two consonants *ch*, cannot *easily* be enunciated in the ordinary time of a short syllable, which its position declares that it is. Almost every reader will be able to appreciate the slight difficulty here; and yet the error is by no means so important as that of the *"And"* in the spondee. By dexterity we *may* pronounce *"such"* in the true time; but the attempt to remedy the rhythmical deficiency of the *And* by drawing it out, merely aggravates the offence against natural enunciation, by directing attention to the offence.

My main object, however, in quoting these lines, is to show that, in spite of the Prosodies, the length of a line is entirely an arbitrary matter. We might divide the commencement of Byron's poem thus:

Know ye the | land where the. |

or thus:

Know ye the | land where the | cypress and. |

or thus:

Know ye the | land where the | cypress and | myrtle are. |

or thus:

Know ye the | land where the | cypress and | myrtle
are | emblems of. |

In short we may give it any division we please, and the lines will be good – provided we have at least *two* feet in a line. As in mathematics two units are required to form number, so rhythm, (from the Greek αριθμος, number,) demands for its formation at least two feet. Beyond doubt, we often see such lines as

Know ye the –
Land where the –

lines of one foot; and our Prosodies admit such; but with impropriety; for common sense would dictate that every so obvious division of a poem as is made by a line, should include within itself all that is necessary for its own comprehension; but in a line of one foot we can have no appreciation of *rhythm*, which depends upon the equality between *two* or more pulsations. The false lines, consisting sometimes of a single cæsura, which are seen in mock Pindaric odes, are of course "rhythmical" only in connection with some other line; and it is this want of independent rhythm which adapts them to the purposes of burlesque alone. Their effect is that of incongruity (the principle of mirth;) for they intrude the blankness of prose amid the harmony of verse.

My second object in quoting Byron's lines, was that of showing how absurd it often is to cite a single line from amid the body of a poem, for the purpose of instancing the perfection or imperfection of the line's rhythm. Were we to see by itself

Know ye the land where the cypress and myrtle,

we might justly condemn it as defective in the final foot, which is equal to only three, instead of being equal to four, short syllables.

In the foot (*flowers ever*) we shall find a further exemplification of the principle in the bastard iambus, bastard trochee, and quick trochee, as I have been at some pains in describing these feet above. All the Prosodies on English verse would insist upon making an elision in "flowers," thus (flow'rs,) but this is nonsense. In the quick trochee (mānȳ are the) occurring in Mr. Cranch's *trochaic* line, we had to equalize the time of the three syllables (*ny, are, the*,) to that of the one *short* syllable whose position they usurp. Accordingly each of these syllables is equal to the third of a short syllable, that is to say, the *sixth of a long*. But in Byron's *dactylic* rhythm, we have to equalize the time of the three syllables (*ers, ev, er,*) to that of the one *long* syllable whose position they usurp or, (which is the same thing,) of the *two short*. Therefore the value of each of the syllables (*ers, ev,* and *er*) is the *third of a long*. We enunciate them with only half the rapidity we employ in enunciating the three final syllables of the quick trochee – which latter is a rare foot. The *"flowers ever,"* on the contrary, is as common in the dactylic rhythm as is the *bastard* trochee in the trochaic, or the bastard iambus in the iambic. We may as well accent it with the curve of the crescent to the right, and call it a *bastard dactyl.* A *bastard anapæst*, whose nature I now need be at no trouble in explaining, will of course occur, now and then, in an anapæstic rhythm.

The object of what we call *scansion* is the distinct making of the rhythmical flow. Scansion without accents or perpendicular lines between the feet – that is to say scansion *by* the voice only – is scansion *to* the ear only; and all very good in its way. The written scansion addresses the ear through the eye. In either case the object is the distinct making of the rhythmical, musical, or reading flow. There *can* be no other object and there is none. Of course, then, the scansion and the reading flow should go hand in hand. The former must agree with the latter. The former represents and expresses the latter; and is good or bad as it truly or falsely represents and expresses it. If by the written scansion of a line we are not enabled to perceive any rhythm or music in the line, then either the line is unrhythmical or the scansion false. Apply all this to the English lines which we have quoted, at various points, in the course of this article. It will be found that the scansion exactly conveys the rhythm, and thus thoroughly fulfils the only purpose for which scansion is required.

But let the scansion *of the schools* be applied to the Greek and Latin verse, and what result do we find? – that the verse is one thing and the scansion quite another. The ancient verse, *read* aloud, is in general musical, and occasionally *very* musical. *Scanned* by the Prosodial rules we can, for the most part, make nothing of it whatever. In the case of the English verse, the more emphatically we dwell on the divisions between the feet, the more distinct is our perception of the kind of rhythm intended. In the case of the Greek and Latin, the more we dwell the *less* distinct is this perception. To make this clear by an example:

> Mæcenas, atavis edite regibus,
> O, et præsidium et dulce decus meum,
> Sunt quos curriculo pulverem Olympicum
> Collegisse juvat, metaque fervidis
> Evitata rotis, palmaque nobilis
> Terrarum dominos evehit ad Deos.

Now in *reading* these lines, there is scarcely one person in a thousand who, if even ignorant of Latin, will not immediately feel and appreciate their flow – their music. A prosodist, however, informs the public that the *scansion* runs thus:

Mæce | nas ata | vis | edite | regibus |
O, et | præsidi' | et | dulce de | cus meum |
Sunt quos | curricu | lo | pulver' O | lympicum |
Colle | gisse ju | vat | metaque | fervidis |
Evi | tato ro | tis | palmaque | nobilis |
Terra | rum domi | nos | evehit | ad Deos. |

Now I do not deny that we get a *certain sort* of music from the lines if we read them according to this scansion, but I wish to call attention to the fact that this scansion and the certain sort of music which grows out of it, are entirely at war not only with the reading flow which any ordinary person would normally give the lines, but with the reading flow universally given them, and never denied them, by even the most obstinate and stolid of scholars.

And now these questions are forced upon us – "Why exists this discrepancy between the modern verse with its scansion, and the ancient verse with its scansion?" – "Why, in the former case, are there agreement and representation, while in the latter there is neither the one nor the other?" or, to come to the point, – "How are we to reconcile the ancient verse with the scholastic scansion of it?" This absolutely necessary conciliation – shall we bring it about by supposing the scholastic scansion wrong because the ancient verse is right, or by maintaining that the ancient verse is wrong because the scholastic scansion is not to be gainsaid?

Were we to adopt the latter mode of arranging the difficulty, we might, in some measure, at least simplify the expression of the arrangement by putting it thus – Because the pedants have no eyes, therefore the old poets had no ears.

"But," say the gentlemen without the eyes, "the scholastic scansion, although certainly not handed down to us in form from the old poets themselves (the gentlemen without the ears,) is nevertheless deduced, Baconially, from certain facts which are supplied us by careful observation of the old poems."

And let us illustrate this strong position by an example from an American poet – who must be a poet of some eminence, or he will not answer the purpose. Let us take Mr. Alfred B. Street. I remember these two lines of his:

> His sinuous path, by blazes, wound
> Among trunks grouped in myriads round.

With the *sense* of these lines I have nothing to do. When a poet is in a "fine phrensy" he may as well imagine a large forest as a small one – and "by blazes!" is *not* intended for an oath. My concern is with the rhythm, which is iambic.

Now let us suppose that, a thousand years hence, when the "American language" is dead, a learned prosodist should be deducing from "careful observation" of our best poets, a system of scansion for our poetry. And let us suppose that this prosodist had so little dependence in the generality and immutability of the laws of Nature, as to assume in the outset, that, because we lived a thousand years before his time and made use of steam-engines instead of mesmeric balloons, we must therefore have had a *very* singular fashion of mouthing our vowels, and altogether of hudsonizing our verse. And let us suppose that with these and other fundamental propositions carefully put away in his brain, he should arrive at the line,

Among | trunks grouped | in my | riads round.

Finding it in an obviously iambic rhythm, he would divide it as above, and observing that "trunks" made the first member of an iambus, he would call it short, as Mr. Street intended it to be. Now farther: – if instead of admitting the possibility that Mr. Street, (who by that time would be called Street simply, just as we say

Homer) – that Mr. Street might have been in the habit of writing carelessly, as the poets of the prosodist's own era did, and as all poets will do (on account of being geniuses) – instead of admitting this, suppose the learned scholar should make a "rule" and put it in a book, to the effect that, in the American verse, the vowel *u, when found embedded among nine consonants,* was *short.* What, under such circumstances, would the sensible people of the scholar's day have a right not only to think, but to say of that scholar? – why, that he was "a fool, – by blazes!"

I have put an extreme case, but it strikes at the root of the error. The "rules" are grounded in "authority" – and this "authority" – can any one tell us what it means? or can any one suggest anything that it may *not* mean? Is it not clear that the "scholar" above referred to, might as readily have deduced from authority a totally false system as a partially true one? To deduce from authority a consistent prosody of the ancient metres would indeed have been within the limits of the barest possibility; and the task has *not* been accomplished, for the reason that it demands a species of ratiocination altogether out of keeping with the brain of a bookworm. A rigid scrutiny will show that the very few "rules" which have not as many exceptions as examples, are those which have, by accident, their true bases not in authority, but in the omniprevalent laws of syllabification; such, for example, as the rule which declares a vowel before two consonants to be long.

In a word, the gross confusion and antagonism of the scholastic prosody, as well as its marked inapplicability to the reading flow of the rhythms it pretends to illustrate, are attributable, first to the utter absence of natural principle as a guide in the investigations which have been undertaken by inadequate men; and secondly to the neglect of the obvious consideration that the ancient poems, which have been the *criteria* throughout, were the work of men who must have written as loosely, and with as little definitive system, as ourselves.

Southern Literary Messenger, October–November 1848

LETTER TO B——[1]

It has been said that a good critique on a poem may be written by one who is no poet himself. This, according to *your* idea and *mine* of poetry, I feel to be false – the less poetical the critic, the less just the critique, and the converse. On this account, and becuse there are but few B——'s in the world, I would be as much ashamed of the world's good opinion as proud of your own. Another than yourself might here observe, "Shakspeare is in possession of the world's good opinion, and yet Shakspeare is the greatest of poets. It appears then that the world judge correctly, why should you be ashamed of their favorable judgment?" The difficulty lies in the interpretation of the word "judgment" or "opinion." The opinion is the world's, truly, but it may be called theirs as a man would call a book his, having bought it; he did not write the book, but it is his; they did not originate the opinion, but it is theirs. A fool, for example, thinks Shakspeare a great poet – yet the fool has never read Shakspeare. But the fool's neighbor, who is a step higher on the Andes of the mind, whose head (that is to say his more exalted thought) is too far above

---

1 These detached passages form part of the preface to a small volume printed some years ago for private circulation. They have vigor and much originality – but of course we shall not be called upon to endorse all the writer's opinions. – *Ed.*

the fool to be seen or understood, but whose feet (by which I mean his every-day actions) are sufficiently near to be discerned, and by means of which that superiority is ascertained, which *but* for them would never have been discovered – this neighbor asserts that Shakspeare is a great poet – the fool believes him, and it is henceforward his *opinion*. This neighbor's own opinion has, in like manner, been adopted from one above *him*, and so, ascendingly, to a few gifted individuals, who kneel around the summit, beholding, face to face, the master spirit who stands upon the pinnacle.

*   *   *

You are aware of the great barrier in the path of an American writer. He is read, if at all, in preference to the combined and established wit of the world. I say established; for it is with literature as with law or empire – an established name is an estate in tenure, or a throne in possession. Besides, one might suppose that books, like their authors, improve by travel – their having crossed the sea is, with us, so great a distinction. Our antiquaries abandon time for distance; our very fops glance from the binding to the bottom of the title-page, where the mystic characters which spell London, Paris, or Genoa, are precisely so many letters of recommendation.

*   *   *

I mentioned just now a vulgar error as regards criticism. I think the notion that no poet can form a correct estimate of his own writings is another. I remarked before, that in proportion to the poetical talent, would be the justice of a critique upon poetry. Therefore, a bad poet would, I grant, make a false critique, and his self-love would infallibly bias his little judgment in his favor; but a poet, who is indeed a poet, could not, I think, fail of making a just critique. Whatever should be deducted on the score of self-love, might be replaced on account of his intimate acquaintance with the subject; in short, we have more instances of false criticism than of just, where one's own writings are the test, simply because we have more bad poets than good. There are of course many objections to what I say: Milton is a great example of the contrary; but his opinion with respect to the Paradise Regained, is by no means fairly ascertained. By what trivial circumstances men are often led to assert what they do not really believe! Perhaps an inadvertent word has descended to posterity. But, in fact, the Paradise Regained is little, if at all, inferior to the Paradise Lost, and is only supposed so to be, because men do not like epics, whatever they may say to the contrary, and reading those of Milton in their natural order, are too much wearied with the first to derive any pleasure from the second.

I dare say Milton preferred Comus to either – if so – justly.

*   *   *

As I am speaking of poetry, it will not be amiss to touch slightly upon the most singular heresy in its modern history – the heresy of what is called very foolishly, the Lake School. Some years ago I might have been induced, by an occasion like the present, to attempt a formal refutation of their doctrine; at present it would be a work of supererogation. The wise must bow to the wisdom of such men as Coleridge and Southey, but being wise, have laughed at poetical theories so prosaically exemplified.

Aristotle, with singular assurance, has declared poetry the most philosophical of all writing[1] – but it required a Wordsworth to pronounce it the most metaphysical. He seems to think that the end of poetry is, or should be, instruction – yet it is a truism that the end of our existence is happiness; if so, the end of every separate part of our existence – every thing connected with our existence should be still happiness. Therefore the end of instruction should be happiness; and happiness is another name for pleasure; – therefore the end of instruction should be pleasure: yet we see the above mentioned opinion implies precisely the reverse.

1 Spoudiotaton kai philosophikotaton genos.

To proceed: ceteris paribus, he who pleases, is of more importance to his fellow men than he who instructs, since utility is happiness, and pleasure is the end already obtained which instruction is merely the means of obtaining.

I see no reason, then, why our metaphysical poets should plume themselves so much on the utility of their works, unless indeed they refer to instruction with eternity in view; in which case, sincere respect for their piety would not allow me to express my contempt for their judgment; contempt which it would be difficult to conceal, since their writings are professedly to be understood by the few, and it is the many who stand in need of salvation. In such case I should no doubt be tempted to think of the devil in Melmoth, who labors indefatigably through three octavo volumes, to accomplish the destruction of one or two souls, while any common devil would have demolished one or two thousand.

* * *

Against the subtleties which would make poetry a study – not a passion – it becomes the metaphysician to reason – but the poet to protest. Yet Wordsworth and Coleridge are men in years; the one imbued in contemplation from his childhood, the other a giant in intellect and learning. The diffidence, then, with which I venture to dispute their authority, would be over-whelming, did

I not feel, from the bottom of my heart, that learning has little to do with the imagination − intellect with the passions − or age with poetry.

*   *   *

"Trifles, like straws, upon the surface flow,
He who would search for pearls must dive below,"

are lines which have done much mischief. As regards the greater truths, men oftener err by seeking them at the bottom than at the top; the depth lies in the huge abysses where wisdom is sought − not in the palpable palaces where she is found. The ancients were not always right in hiding the goddess in a well: witness the light which Bacon has thrown upon philosophy; witness the principles of our divine faith − that moral mechanism by which the simplicity of a child may overbalance the wisdom of a man.

We see an instance of Coleridge's liability to err, in his Biographia Literaria − professedly his literary life and opinions, but, in fact, a treatise *de omni scibili et quibusdam aliis*. He goes wrong by reason of his very profundity, and of his error we have a natural type in the contemplation of a star. He who regards it directly and intensely sees, it is true, the star, but it is the star without a ray − while he who surveys it less inquisitively is conscious of all for which the star is useful to us below − its brilliancy and its beauty.

* * *

As to Wordsworth, I have no faith in him. That he had, in youth, the feelings of a poet I believe – for there are glimpses of extreme delicacy in his writings – (and delicacy is the poet's own kingdom – his *El Dorado*) – but they have the appearance of a better day recollected; and glimpses, at best, are little evidence of present poetic fire – we know that a few straggling flowers spring up daily in the crevices of the glacier.

He was to blame in wearing away his youth in contemplation with the end of poetizing in his manhood. With the increase of his judgment the light which should make it apparent has faded away. His judgment consequently is too correct. This may not be understood, – but the old Goths of Germany would have understood it, who used to debate matters of importance to their State twice, once when drunk, and once when sober – sober that they might not be deficient in formality – drunk lest they should be destitute of vigor.

The long wordy discussions by which he tries to reason us into admiration of his poetry, speak very little in his favor: they are full of such assertions as this – (I have opened one of his volumes at random) "Of genius the only proof is the act of doing well what is worthy to be done, and what was never done before" – indeed!

then it follows that in doing what is *un*worthy to be done, or what *has* been done before, no genius can be evinced: yet the picking of pockets is an unworthy act, pockets have been picked time immemorial, and Barrington, the pick-pocket, in point of genius, would have thought hard of a comparison with William Wordsworth, the poet.

Again – in estimating the merit of certain poems, whether they be Ossian's or M'Pherson's, can surely be of little consequence, yet, in order to prove their worthlessness, Mr. W. has expended many pages in the controversy. *Tantæne animis?* Can great minds descend to such absurdity? But worse still: that he may bear down every argument in favor of these poems, he triumphantly drags forward a passage, in his abomination of which he expects the reader to sympathize. It is the beginning of the epic poem *"Temora."* "The blue waves of Ullin roll in light; the green hills are covered with day; trees shake their dusky heads in the breeze." And this – this gorgeous, yet simple imagery – where all is alive and panting with immortality – this – William Wordsworth, the author of Peter Bell, has *selected* for his contempt. We shall see what better he, in his own person, has to offer. Imprimis:

> "And now she's at the pony's head,
> And now she's at the pony's tail,

On that side now, and now on this,
And almost stifled her with bliss –
A few sad tears does Betty shed,
She pats the pony where or when
She knows not: happy Betty Foy!
O Johnny! never mind the Doctor!"

Secondly:

"The dew was falling fast, the – stars began to blink,
I heard a voice, it said – drink, pretty creature, drink;
And looking o'er the hedge, be – fore me I espied
A snow-white mountain lamb with a – maiden at its
    side,
No other sheep were near, the lamb was all alone,
And by a slender cord was – tether'd to a stone."

Now we have no doubt this is all true; we *will* believe
it, indeed we will, Mr. W. Is it sympathy for the sheep
you wish to excite? I love a sheep from the bottom of my
heart.

*   *   *

But there *are* occasions, dear B——, there are
occasions when even Wordsworth is reasonable. Even
Stamboul, it is said, shall have an end, and the most
unlucky blunders must come to a conclusion. Here is an
extract from his preface –

"Those who have been accustomed to the phrase-ology of modern writers, if they persist in reading this book to a conclusion (*impossible!*) will, no doubt, have to struggle with feelings of awkwardness; (ha! ha! ha!) they will look round for poetry (ha! ha! ha! ha!) and will be induced to inquire by what species of courtesy these attempts have been permitted to assume that title." Ha! ha! ha! ha! ha!

Yet let not Mr. W. despair; he has given immortality to a wagon, and the bee Sophocles has transmitted to eternity a sore toe, and dignified a tragedy with a chorus of turkeys.

*   *   *

Of Coleridge I cannot speak but with reverence. His towering intellect! his gigantic power! He is one more evidence of the fact "que la plupart des sectes ont raison dans une bonne partie de ce qu'elles avancent, mais non pas en ce qu'elles nient." He has imprisoned his own conceptions by the barrier he has erected against those of others. It is lamentable to think that such a mind should be buried in metaphysics, and, like the Nyctanthes, waste its perfume upon the night alone. In reading his poetry I tremble – like one who stands upon a volcano, conscious, from the very darkness bursting from the crater, of the fire and the light that are weltering below.

* * *

What is Poetry? – Poetry! that Proteus-like idea, with as many appellations as the nine-titled Corcyra! Give me, I demanded of a scholar some time ago, give me a definition of poetry? "Tres-volontiers," – and he proceeded to his library, brought me a Dr. Johnson, and overwhelmed me with a definition. Shade of the immortal Shakspeare! I imagined to myself the scowl of your spiritual eye upon the profanity of that scurrilous Ursa Major. Think of poetry, dear B——, think of poetry, and then think of – Dr. Samuel Johnson! Think of all that is airy and fairy-like, and then of all that is hideous and unwieldy; think of his huge bulk, the Elephant! and then – and then think of the Tempest – the Midsummer Night's Dream – Prospero – Oberon – and Titania!

* * *

A poem, in my opinion, is opposed to a work of science by having, for its *immediate* object, pleasure, not truth; to romance, by having for its object an *indefinite* instead of a *definite* pleasure, being a poem only so far as this object is attained; romance presenting perceptible images with definite, poetry with *in*definite sensations, to which end music is an *essential*, since the comprehension of sweet sound is our most indefinite conception. Music, when combined with a pleasurable idea, is poetry; music without the idea is simply music; the idea without the music is prose from its very definitiveness.

What was meant by the invective against him who had no music in his soul?

* * *

To sum up this long rigmarole, I have, dear B——, what you no doubt perceive, for the metaphysical poets, *as* poets, the most sovereign contempt. That they have followers proves nothing –

No Indian prince has to his palace
More followers than a thief to the gallows.

Southern Literary Messenger, July 1836

PREFACE

(Tamerlane and Other Poems – 1827)

The greater part of the Poems which compose this little volume, were written in the year 1821-2, when the author had not completed his fourteenth year. They were of course not intended for publication; why they are now published concerns no one but himself. Of the smaller pieces very little need be said: they perhaps savour too much of Egotism; but they were written by one too young to have any knowledge of the world but from his own breast.

In Tamerlane, he has endeavoured to expose the folly of even *risking* the best feelings of the heart at the shrine of Ambition. He is conscious that in this there are many faults, (besides that of the general character of the poem) which he flatters himself he could, with little trouble, have corrected, but unlike many of his predecessors, has been too fond of his early productions to amend them in his *old age*.

He will not say that he is indifferent as to the success of these Poems – it might stimulate him to other attempts – but he can safely assert that failure will not at all influence him in a resolution already adopted. This is challenging criticism – let it be so. *Nos hæc novimus esse nihil.*

PREFACE

(The Raven and Other Poems – 1845)

These trifles are collected and republished chiefly with a view to their redemption from the many improvements to which they have been subjected while going at random "the rounds of the press." If what I have written is to circulate at all, I am naturally anxious that it should circulate as I wrote it. In defence of my own taste, nevertheless, it is incumbent upon me to say, that I think nothing in this volume of much value to the public, or very creditable to myself. Events not to be controlled have prevented me from making, at any time, any serious effort in what, under happier circumstances, would have been the field of my choice. With me poetry has been not a purpose, but a passion; and the passions should be held in reverence; they must not – they cannot at will be excited with an eye to the paltry compensations, or the more paltry commendations, of mankind.

E. A. P.

We have said that Mr. Longfellow's conception of the *aims* of poesy is erroneous; and that thus, laboring at a disadvantage, he does violent wrong to his own high powers; and now the question is, what *are* his ideas of the aims of the Muse, as we gather these ideas from the *general* tendency of his poems? It will be at once evident that, imbued with the peculiar spirit of German song (a pure conventionality) he regards the inculcation of a *moral* as essential. Here we find it necessary to repeat that we have reference only to the *general* tendency of his compositions; for there are some magnificent exceptions, where, as if by accident, he has permitted his genius to get the better of his conventional prejudice. But didacticism is the prevalent *tone* of his song. His invention, his imagery, his all, is made subservient to the elucidation of some one or more points (but rarely of more than one) which he looks upon as *truth*. And that this mode of procedure will find stern defenders should never excite surprise, so long as the world is full to overflowing with cant and conventicles. There are men who will scramble on all fours through the muddiest sloughs of vice to pick up a single apple of virtue. There are things called men who, so long as the sun rolls, will greet with snuffling huzzas every figure that takes upon itself the semblance of truth, even although the figure, in itself only a "stuffed Paddy," be as much out of place as a toga on the statue of Washington, or out of season as rabbits in the days of the dog-star.

Now with as deep a reverence for "the true" as ever inspired the bosom of mortal man, we would limit, in many respects, its modes of inculcation. We would limit to enforce them. We would not render them impotent by dissipation. The demands of truth are severe. She has no sympathy with the myrtles. All that is indispensible in song is all with which she has nothing to do. To deck her in gay robes is to render her a harlot. It is but making her a flaunting paradox to wreathe her in gems and flowers. Even in stating this our present proposition, we verify our own words – we feel the necessity, in enforcing this *truth*, of descending from metaphor. Let us then be simple and distinct. To convey "the true" we are required to dismiss from the attention all inessentials. We must be perspicuous, precise, terse. We need concentration rather than expansion of mind. We must be calm, unimpassioned, unexcited – in a word, we must be in that peculiar mood which, as nearly as possible, is the exact converse of the poetical. He must be blind indeed who cannot perceive the radical and chasmal difference between the truthful and the poetical modes of inculcation. He must be grossly wedded to conventionalisms who, in spite of this difference, shall still

243

attempt to reconcile the obstinate oils and waters of Poetry and Truth.

Dividing the world of mind into its most obvious and immediately recognisable distinctions, we have the pure intellect, taste, and the moral sense. We place *taste* between the intellect and the moral sense, because it is just this intermediate space which, in the mind, it occupies. It is the connecting link in the triple chain. It serves to sustain a mutual intelligence between the extremes. It appertains, in strict appreciation, to the former, but is distinguished from the latter by so faint a difference, that Aristotle has not hesitated to class some of its operations among the Virtues themselves. But the *offices* of the trio are broadly marked. Just as conscience, or the moral sense, recognises duty; just as the intellect deals with *truth*; so is it the part of taste alone to inform us of BEAUTY. And Poesy is the handmaiden but of Taste. Yet we would not be misunderstood. This handmaiden is not forbidden to moralise – in her own fashion. She is not forbidden to depict – but to reason and preach, of virtue. As, of this latter, conscience recognises the obligation, so intellect teaches the expediency, while taste contents herself with displaying the beauty: waging war with vice merely on the ground of its inconsistency with fitness, harmony, proportion – in a word with το χαλον.

An important condition of man's immortal nature is

thus, plainly, the sense of the Beautiful. This it is which ministers to his delight in the manifold forms and colors and sounds and sentiments amid which he exists. And, just as the eyes of Amaryllis are repeated in the mirror, or the living lily in the lake, so is the mere *record* of these forms and colors and sounds and sentiments – so is their mere oral or written repetition a duplicate source of delight. But this repetition is not Poesy. He who shall merely sing with whatever rapture, in however harmonious strains, or with however vivid a truth of imitation, of the sights and sounds which greet him in common with all mankind – he, we say, has yet failed to prove his divine title. There is still a longing unsatisfied, which he has been impotent to fulfil. There is still a thirst unquenchable, which to allay he has shown us no crystal springs. This burning thirst belongs to the *immortal* essence of man's nature. It is equally a consequence and an indication of his perennial life. It is the desire of the moth for the star. It is not the mere appreciation of the beauty before us. It is a wild effort to reach the beauty above. It is a forethought of the loveliness to come. It is a passion to be satiated by no sublunary sights, or sounds, or sentiments, and the soul thus athirst strives to allay its fever in futile efforts at *creation*. Inspired with a prescient ecstasy of the beauty beyond the grave, it struggles by multiform novelty of combination among the things and thoughts of Time, to anticipate some portion of that loveliness whose very elements, perhaps, appertain solely to Eternity. And the result of such effort, on the part of souls fittingly constituted, is alone what mankind have agreed to denominate Poetry.

We say this with little fear of contradiction. Yet the spirit of our assertion must be more heeded than the letter. Mankind have *seemed* to define Poesy in a thousand, and in a thousand conflicting definitions. But the war is one only of words. Induction is as well applicable to this subject as to the most palpable and utilitarian; and by its sober processes we find that, in respect to compositions which have been really received as poems, the *imaginative*, or, more popularly, the creative portions *alone* have ensured them to be so received. Yet these works, on accounts of these portions, having once been so received and so named, it has happened, naturally and inevitably, that other portions totally unpoetic have not only come to be regarded by the popular voice as poetic, but have been made to serve as false standards of perfection, in the adjustment of other poetical claims. Whatever has been found in whatever has been received as a poem, has been blindly regarded as *ex statû* poetic. And this is a species of gross error which scarcely could have made its way into any less intangible topic. In fact that license which appertains to the Muse herself, it has been thought decorous, if not sagacious to indulge, in all examination of her character.

Poesy is thus seen to be a response – unsatisfactory it is true – but still in some measure a response, to a natural and irrepressible demand. Man being what he is, the time could never have been in which Poesy was not. Its first element is the thirst for supernal BEAUTY – a beauty which is not afforded the soul by any existing collocation of earth's forms – a beauty which, perhaps, *no possible* combination of these forms would fully produce. Its second element is the attempt to satisfy this thirst by *novel* combinations among those forms of beauty which already exist – or by novel combinations *of those combinations which our predecessors, toiling in chase of the same phantom, have already set in order.* We thus clearly deduce the *novelty*, the *originality*, the *invention*, the *imagination*, or lastly the *creation* of BEAUTY, (for the terms as here employed are synonimous) as the essence of all Poesy. Nor is this idea so much at variance with ordinary opinion as, at first sight, it may appear. A multitude of antique dogmas on this topic will be found, when divested of extrinsic speculation, to be easily resoluble into the definition now proposed. We do nothing more than present tangibly the vague clouds of the world's idea. We recognize the idea itself floating, unsettled, indefinite, in every attempt which has yet been made to circumscribe the conception of "Poesy" in words. A striking instance of this is observable in the fact that no definition exists, in which either "the beautiful," or some one of those qualities which we have above designated synonimously with "creation," has not been pointed out as the *chief* attribute of the Muse. "Invention," however, or "imagination," is by far more commonly insisted upon. The word πσημσις itself (creation) speaks volumes upon this point. Neither will it be amiss here to mention Count Bielfeld's definition of poetry as *"L'art d'exprimer les pensées par la fiction."* With this definition (of which the philosophy is profound to a certain extent) the German terms *Dichtkunst*, the art of fiction, and *Dichten*, to feign, which are used for *"poetry"* and *"to make verses,"* are in full and remarkable accordance. It is, nevertheless, in the *combination* of the two omni-prevalent ideas that the novelty and, we believe, the force of our own proposition is to be found.

So far, we have spoken of Poesy as of an abstraction alone. As such, it is obvious that it may be applicable in various moods. The sentiment may develop itself in Sculpture, in Painting, in Music, or otherwise. But our present business is with its development in words – that development to which, in practical acceptation, the world has agreed to limit the term. And at this point there is one consideration which induces us to pause. We cannot make up our minds to admit (as some have admitted) the inessentiality of rhythm. On the contrary, the universality of its use in the earliest poetical efforts of all mankind would be sufficient to assure us, not merely of its congeniality with the Muse, or of its adaptation to her purposes, but of its elementary and indispensible importance. But here we must, perforce, content ourselves with mere suggestion; for this topic is of a character which would lead us too far. We have already spoken of Music as one of the moods of poetical development. It is in Music, perhaps, that the soul most nearly attains that end upon which we have commented – the creation of supernal beauty. It may be, indeed, that this august aim is here even partially or imperfectly attained, *in fact*. The *elements* of that beauty which is felt in sound, *may be* the mutual or common heritage of Earth and Heaven. In the soul's struggles at combination it is thus not impossible that a harp may strike notes not unfamiliar to the angels. And in this view the wonder may well be less that all attempts at defining the character or sentiment of the deeper musical impressions, has been found absolutely futile. Contenting ourselves, therefore, with the firm conviction, that music (in its modifications of rhythm and rhyme) is of so vast a moment in Poesy, as *never* to be neglected by him who is truly poetical – is of so mighty a force in furthering the great aim intended that he is mad who rejects its assistance – content with this idea we shall not pause to maintain its absolute essentiality, for the mere sake of rounding a definition. We will but add, at this point, that the highest possible development of the

Poetical Sentiment is to be found in the union of song with music, in its popular sense. The old Bards and Minnesingers possessed, in the fullest perfection, the finest and truest elements of Poesy; and Thomas Moore, singing his own ballads, is but putting the final touch to their completion as poems.

To recapitulate, then, we would define in brief the Poetry of words as the *Rhythmical Creation of Beauty*. Beyond the limits of Beauty its province does not extend. Its sole arbiter is Taste. With the Intellect or with the Conscience it has only collateral relations. It has no dependence, unless incidentally, upon either Duty or *Truth*. That our definition will necessarily exclude much of what, through a supine toleration, has been hitherto ranked as poetical, is a matter which affords us not even momentary concern. We address but the thoughtful, and heed only their approval – with our own. If our suggestions are truthful, then "after many days" shall they be understood as truth, even though found in contradiction of *all* that has been hitherto so understood. If false shall we not be the first to bid them die?

INDEX OF FIRST LINES